Consensual Christianity

Developing a Relationship with God that is Biblical, Fruitful, and Eternal

Second Edition

J. Nathaniel Blizzard

Copyright Page:

Dedication

This book is dedicated to my great-grandmother, Carrie Blizzard.

"His eye is on the sparrow, and I know He watches me."

Special Thanks

I would like to say thank you to a very special group of people who have helped me tremendously throughout this process. Thank you Mitchel Walker for being my friend and sounding board, and ensuring I did not become a heretic. Thank you D. J. Tuang for designing all of my cover art and logos. You have been my best friend for many years and you are truly the most talented person I know. Thank you Jennifer Walker for your diligence in proofing my work and making sure I did not upset any of my past English teachers. And last, but not least, I owe a great deal of gratitude to my wife. Thank you Rashidah for allowing me to share stories about our life, giving me the time to write this book, for your love for me, and your patience throughout this process. I love you.

Second Edition

I chose to write a second edition of *Consensual Christianity* because I felt the need to expound on some things. After writing the first edition, which was my very first book by the way, I realized that there were some things that sounded better in my head than they did on paper, and that there were some things that I should have clarified in greater detail to avoid any confusion.

I must say that I am extremely proud of this book. I have told several people close to me that I believe God has used this book as a means of teaching me how to have a better relationship with Him and how to overcome some of my personal obstacles. I often refer back to what I have written when I am going through a difficult situation. I want to encourage you to read this book with an open mind and an open heart. Write in the book, take notes, journal about the things God is teaching you as you read the book, and most importantly apply the lessons learned to your life. This book does not have any transformative power. Only the Bible can make that claim. However, I believe that this book can have a significant impact on your life.

Understanding the importance of having a relationship with God is not only essential, it is also empowering. God can and will meet you where you are if you allow Him. Jesus said that He came so we could have life more abundantly. There is no greater place of abundance than being in a personal relationship with the Savior of the world. If you lack hope, God can give you hope. If you lack peace, God can give you peace. If you lack joy,

God can give you joy. No matter what your circumstances may be, God can and will see you through. He has promised to never leave you nor forsake you. Trust in God! I hope and pray that the Lord bless you richly as you embark on the wonderful journey of developing a relationship with Him!

Preface

I was raised in church, attended a Christian school and eventually went to a Bible college. I went on mission trips, prayed for the sick, and shared the Gospel. I was a member at a vibrant church, part of a wonderful youth group, and even served at summer camp. I lived in a home with a godly mother and a grandmother who prayed for me constantly. That sounds like a good foundation, doesn't it? Well, a good foundation doesn't always equal a sturdy house, at least not initially.

Let me tell you a little bit more about myself. I have three wonderful children, all conceived out of wedlock. I committed numerous sins, worst of all turning my back on God. The funny part is that while all of this was going on, I constantly wondered how I could have fallen so far. After all, I was supposed to be a minister, called by God to share His Word and teach His people how to live in a manner that pleases Him. I knew the Scriptures, I could quote a lot of Scriptures from memory, but I found myself doing all the things that I had despised for so long. All of the things that my mother worked so hard to shield me from and the things that my youth pastor had constantly warned me about were now a major part of my everyday life. I was broken, constantly looking to be fixed in all the wrong places. I found myself tired and depressed, battling sexual addiction and in a fight for my life. Three things that I am forever grateful for are that I lived through the whole process, that I learned what was truly missing in my life, and the redeeming, restoring blood of Jesus Christ.

I was not the Christ-follower that I thought I was. I was a church follower. All the while I believed that I was okay because I was doing "God's work." Even in the midst of doing "God's work," I always felt like something was missing, something just wasn't quite right. I had watched so many of my close friends fall away from God and I vowed that it would never happen to me, but it did. For 8 years I couldn't even walk into a church because of guilt. I did not think that God would want me back and I felt like I was too broken for God to fix. As a teen, I often thought to myself "God must really want to use me, why else would He give me all that He has given me?" He gave me a Christian education, a wonderful church, a godly mother, and godly friends. I was destined to do great things for God; after all, to him whom much is given, much is required.

In 1997, when I was 20 years old, something happened that changed my life forever. Earlier that year I enrolled in college at Liberty University, scheduled to start in the fall semester. My mother made sure that my tuition was covered and even helped me get a car. After being at Liberty for a short time, I made a bizarre and costly decision. I quit school and moved back home with my mother. Once I got settled in at home I enrolled in the local community college and applied for a job at a local department store. This is where the whirlwind of sin and separation from God all began. This was the beginning of the fornication and idolatry that kept me away from God for more than eight years.

There are not very many positive things that happened

during that period. I did gain 3 wonderful children, a lifetime of experiences and wisdom, and the answer to my problem, an answer to the reason why things never seemed quite right, even when I was doing "God's work." My problem was that my relationship was with the church, the people in the church, and the work I did for the church, but I had never bothered to develop a personal relationship with God. Life was good while I was surrounded by the people at the church but, once I left that environment, the wave of temptation came. It was more like a tsunami and it hit me full force. I had built my house upon the sand instead of on the Rock, and I got swept away. Feeling hopeless, worthless, and guilt ridden, I nearly drowned. I reached a point where my whole life was in shambles. For years I battle serious depression and anxiety issues that eventually led to thoughts and attempts of suicide. It was at the end of that period that I realized how much I needed God. I needed a relationship with Him. This realization did not change things overnight, but it did expose the void in my life and highlight my glaring misunderstanding of what being a Christian truly means. Just like every relationship, it grows day by day. It has its ups and downs. Sometimes I feel really close to God, sometimes I don't. Although we strive daily to be like Jesus we are not now, nor will we ever be, perfect while we occupy our earthly bodies. My prayer is that this book helps you to understand the importance of a relationship with God and why our focus has to remain on Him. Whether you are in the midst of the storm, the eye of the storm, or if you see nothing but blue skies, God is with you and

He promises to never leave you nor forsake you. All you have to do is trust in Him and He will see you through. Don't ever allow yourself to get so caught up in doing that you forget how to simply be in His presence.

Table of Contents

Introduction

So where do we begin? Where do all good relationships begin? Attraction, there is always something about that other person that you are attracted to, something that captures your interest. Whether it is looks, personality, vocation, or hobbies, there is always something there to draw you in. Our relationship with God works the same way. What was it that initially drew you to Jesus Christ? You may not realize this, but it was actually Christ that drew you to Himself. In John 12:32, Jesus said, "If I be lifted up from the earth I will draw all men unto me (NKJV)." You may be under the impression that it was you who found God, but it really works the other way around. We make the decision to accept Christ's gift of salvation, but it is the Holy Spirit that convicts us of sin and draws us to the Cross. Now you may be wondering what attraction has to do with all of this. Well, the Holy Spirit uses the people and experiences in our life to draw us to Christ. Maybe it was seeing the love that your parents have for Him or maybe it was being at the bottom of the barrel with nowhere else to go. It could have been a man or woman of God praying for you, sharing their testimony with you, and ultimately introducing you to Him. Regardless of what drew you to Him, here you are, and now you are wondering what to do with this new relationship.

It is interesting to me how Christians, whether rookies or veterans, have trouble maintaining a relationship with someone we claim to love so much. What causes so many believers to "fall in and out of love" with God? Why are we so quick to blame God, get angry with God, and eventually turn our back on God, who promises to never leave us or forsake us? I believe that the answer lies in what we truly know and believe about the God that we serve. Just like a normal relationship, it's hard to trust someone that you don't know very well. Consequently, it is very easy to blame them for things and get angry with them when things don't go the way you think they should. On the flip side, think about that friend that you have, you know the one that you have known since grade school. It's very easy to overlook problems you feel they created, even if you get hurt in the process, even when everything in you and everyone around you are warning you that heartache is on the way. The reason behind that is because you feel that you truly and deeply "know" that person, and you trust them enough to believe that they have your best interests at heart. Trust is the key, and that trust only exists because we have taken the time to get to know that person. Our relationship with God is no different. We have to take the time to get to know Him and learn to trust and believe that He has our best interest at heart. So let's take some time to get a deeper understanding of who God really is, what He expects from us, and what we should expect from Him.

1

Who is this God you speak of?

After these things, the word of the Lord came to Abram in a vision saying,
"Do not be afraid, Abram. I am your shield, your exceedingly great reward.
Genesis 15:1

Consensual Christianity

Prior to developing a personal relationship with God, I always thought that God was an untouchable figurehead of sorts; almost as though He was real but separate from reality. I don't mean that in a disrespectful way. I am just being honest. I'm not even sure if that will make sense to you, but that is the best way I can think of to describe it. God was real; He just wasn't real to me. In hindsight, I realize that I thought and felt that way because I only knew about God on an intellectual level, not a personal one. Since my understanding was intellectual, I was only able to see Him and experience Him in a finite way. My simple human brain could not truly comprehend His greatness. I could only explain Him through tangible things, much like a scientist would try to explain a theory. Therefore, when I talked about God it was in a very impersonal, academic manner. I could tell you what the Bible says about Him, but I could not tell you my personal, experience-based opinion of Him.

This should have been a red flag to me. 1 Peter 3:15 says, *"But sanctify the Lord God in your hearts, and always be ready to give a defense to everyone who asks you a reason for the hope that is in you, with meekness and fear."* The reason for the hope that is in you that Peter is referring to is your personal testimony of Jesus' saving power at work in your life, backed by Biblical truth. I have learned over the years that non-believers are far more interested in my personal story than they are in my ability to quote Scripture. That is not to say that quoting Scripture is bad, but we need to be able to show who God is in our lives and tell what God has done for us in a personal way. We will talk more about the importance of our testimony later in this book but remember that your testimony is powerful, no matter how insignificant it may seem to you. You are a walking, talking demonstration of God's power to heal and to restore. Don't ever be afraid to share who God is to you and what He has done for you!

The purpose of this chapter is to gain a deeper understanding of who God is so we can better relate to Him. Let me be the first to say that no amount of pages in any book can fully express the greatness of our God. The only way to truly know God is to spend time with Him on a consistent basis. You do this by reading His word, spending time in prayer, praising Him, worshipping Him, and by submitting to His will. My goal here is to simply lay a foundation for you to build on as you develop your personal relationship with Him. Remember, a relationship with God is a personal thing, not an intellectual one. You don't need a Ph.D. to understand Him; you just need to spend time with Him. He will reveal Himself to you!

I am warning you up front, this chapter may read more like a lesson from Sunday school or an introductory course at Seminary, but I have a good reason for that. If we truly want to know who God is, we have to go back to the basics in a sense. For some, this chapter may be a review of things you already know. For others, this may be completely new information. In either case, I promise you that this chapter is a very necessary foundation in the process of developing a relationship with God. After all, we must have a clear understanding of just who God is if we ever hope to be in a real relationship with Him. In

Consensual Christianity

this chapter we will look at 5 different relational aspects of God:

1) God, The Creator
2) God, The Alpha and The Omega
3) Yahweh, (Jehovah)
4) God, Our Master
5) God, Our Father

I am sure that we could come up with more aspects of God's nature but for the purposes of developing the relationship, these are the ones we will focus on.

The Creator

What better place is there to start than where it all truly began? Most believers do not realize just how important it is to know God as our Creator. That is why so many profess Christ yet they believe in Darwin's theory of evolution to also be true. Let me start by clarifying a few things. First, we must be sure of our stance on creation. You may be wondering why that is. If we believe the Bible to be the ultimate authority, then every claim that God makes in it must be true. If not, we are left to decide what is true and what is not. Secondly, if evolution is true and we are here by chance, resulting from the Big Bang through billions of years of random changes and adaptations, then it would follow that life itself is decided by chance. Consequently, our choices and decisions are meaningless. Thirdly, if we believe as some do, that God made creation through the process of evolution, then that leads us to the conclusion that this is all by chance and not the design of our loving heavenly Father. Jesus

4

claimed that all that is written in the Law and the Prophets (a reference to what we would consider the Old Testament) is true. If Jesus was wrong about that then how can we be sure of His claims about His deity, His ability to save us, or the fact that He died and rose again? As you can see, our view of creation can and will ultimately determine our view of all of Christianity. Let's dive in and get to know God, the Creator!

In Genesis chapter one, we have an account of how God created the heavens and the earth, the birds and the fish, and eventually Adam and Eve. Man is created in the image and likeness of God:

Let us make man in Our own image, according to Our likeness. Let them have dominion over the fish of the sea, over the birds of the air, and over the cattle, over all the earth and over every creeping thing that creeps on the earth. So God created man in His own image, in the image of God He created him; male and female He created them. [1]

Does that mean that God looks like a human? I don't believe so. I believe it refers to the fact that we have a spirit, just as God is Spirit. It also highlights the fact that we are the only thing in all of creation that has a spirit. If you look at creation, man is the only thing that God actually breathed life into. It is our spirit that gives us free will, the capacity to make decisions, the opportunity to spend eternity with God, and the capability of having a relationship with God while we are here on earth.

[1]   Genesis 1:26-27, NKJV

So why did God create man? Why did He create the earth and the heavens, the birds, and the stars? The answer to that question actually lies in the Book of Revelation; *"You are worthy O Lord to receive glory and honor and power; for You created all things, and for Your pleasure they exist and were created,"(Revelation 4:11)*. You and I were created for God's pleasure. He created us because He wanted to ... plain and simple! We were created to glorify Him, to honor Him, to be a testament of His power, and to be an instrument for His pleasure. Understanding this is important. This will lay the foundation for your relationship with God.

It is with this understanding that we move forward in our relationship with God. Know that God created you on purpose and for a purpose. You are not the result of some cosmic explosion or primordial soup. You were designed by the ultimate Designer. Ephesians 2:10 says that we are God's workmanship, created for good works. You are here for a reason.

The Alpha and the Omega

Of the 5 aspects of God that we are discussing, this is the least noted in the Bible. However, I feel it is one of, if not the most important, aspects of God that we can grab hold of. In the Book of Revelation, when Jesus testifies to the Churches, He says, *"And behold, I am coming quickly, and My reward is with Me, to give to everyone according to his work. I am the Alpha and the Omega, the Beginning and the End, the First and the Last."[2]* God, The Alpha and the Omega, is all encompassing, all knowing, all seeing, all

---

[2]   Revelation 22:12-13, NKJV

hearing, and sovereign; nothing in heaven or on earth happens without His knowledge or His permission.

The Bible gives us the perfect example of God's sovereignty in the Book of Job. The Book of Job starts with Satan standing before God, and God speaking about His servant Job who is a righteous man; one who loves God and shuns evil. Satan then proceeds to tell God that Job is only righteous because He has been blessed. Satan, the accuser of the brethren, then states that if God will remove His hand of blessing from Job, Job will curse God. Now this is where it gets interesting, God allows Satan to take away all that Job has; Job loses all of his property and all of his children. Even in the midst of turmoil, Job remains faithful to God. Satan then returns to God, and God again states that Job is faithful. Satan says that Job's faithfulness is only because God allowed Job to keep his health. God agrees to allow Satan to attack Job's body, but not kill him. Job becomes covered in painful boils from head to toe, but still remains faithful to God.[3]

As people we often assume that Satan has the power to cause sickness, disease, calamity and even death. Although he may possess the ability to do these things, he does not possess the authority. Even Satan must ask God's permission before he can "attack" one of God's children. We must come to the realization that, when trials and tribulations come into our lives, God has allowed it. Now, that does not mean that God wishes bad things for His children. To the contrary, God allows our

---

[3]   Job 1:1 – 2:10, NKJV

Consensual Christianity

faith to be tested because He knows it will result in our spiritual growth and the development of our faith.

This may lead some of you to ask if God tempts us or allows us to be tempted. 1 Corinthians 10:13 says, *"There has no temptation taken you but such as is common to man: but God is faithful, who will not suffer you to be tempted above that you are able; but will with the temptation also make a way to escape, that you may be able to bear it."* God does not tempt us! We are tempted because of our own fleshly desires according to James 1:13-14, *"Let no man say when he is tempted, I am tempted of God: for God cannot be tempted with evil, neither tempts he any man: But every man is tempted, when he is drawn away of his own lust, and enticed."* You must remember that Satan's purpose is to steal, kill, and destroy and as a result to attempt to thwart the plan of God. He does this primarily through deception and using God's word out of context as he did when he tempted Jesus. I used to ask myself, "If God really loves me, why do I keep going through all of this mess?" The answer is that God knows the only way I can become strong spiritually is by exercising my spiritual muscles and learning to truly and fully rely on Him. We may face situations we feel we cannot bear, but we must remember that God has promised to never leave us or forsake us. He will see us through. We may not be able to do it in our own strength, but His strength is perfected in our weakness.

Resisting temptation, praising our way through trials, and marching on through tribulations are what make us strong as Christians. Without these spiritual "exercises" we would never be able to grow as believers. A pastor I know once said that *"God chooses people to be His sign post,"* a testament of His steadfast love even in the midst of adversity. There is nothing glamorous about being a sign post, but there are great rewards if we remain faithful. Remember, God is sovereign, nothing, absolutely nothing happens without His knowledge or His permission. God is always in control!

Yahweh: (Jehovah)

Most of us look at Jehovah as an "Old Testament" God; the God of the children of Israel. We look at how Jehovah delivered the children of Israel out of the land of Egypt and into the land of milk and honey. We see the many wonders and miracles He performed to get them out safely, and we see glimpses of Him as our Father as He disciplined them by not allowing them to enter the Promised Land due to their disobedience and unbelief. It is true; God is only referred to as Jehovah in the Old Testament, but the Bible says that God is the same yesterday, today, and forever. As we develop our relationship with God, it is imperative to know Him as Jehovah because it is in Jehovah that we place our trust, find our shelter, and have our peace. Jehovah is a name that God gave to Himself. The name is a noun and not meant to replace the word "God;" it is God being personal with His people. As Jehovah, we see God reveal Himself in many different ways. He is revealed to us as Jehovah Jireh, which means "The Lord Will Provide" or "The Lord Our Provider." He is also revealed to us as Jehovah Rophe,

Consensual Christianity

"The Lord Our Healer," and Jehovah Shalom, "The Lord Our Peace" just to name a few.

Jehovah is holy and should be respected and revered. *"That they may know You, whose name alone; Jehovah, are the Most High over all the earth."*[4] Jehovah is our strength, our provider, and our peace. Jehovah is the God of all that we need. In Him we live and move and have our being. *"Behold God is my salvation, I will trust and not be afraid. For Jehovah, the Lord, is my strength and song, He also has become my salvation."*[5] As we develop our relationship with God, we begin to rely on Him more and more. I believe that He reveals His ability and desire to care for us through the different aspects of Jehovah. God indeed is our sustenance; the more you trust in Him, the more He will provide for you. God is a gentleman, and will not force Himself on you. He wants you to accept Him. He has already accepted you. The many aspects of Jehovah, or God's character revealed as Jehovah, demonstrate God's willingness and desire to be personal with and connected to His people. He is not an angry over-lord as some would portray Him, or an unconcerned deity. He personally and sincerely loves you, desires to care for you, and longs to spend time with you.

"Trust in the LORD forever, For the Lord God is an everlasting rock."[6]

Our Master

Master: 1) A male teacher. 2) On having authority over

---

4   Psalm 83:18, NKJV
5   Isaiah 12:2, NKJV
6   Isaiah 26:4, ESV

10

Chapter 1

another. 3) One having control. 4) The employer especially of a servant. 5) The male head of a household. 6) A victor or conqueror.[7]

"And whatever you do (in word or deed), do it heartily, as unto the Lord and not to men (as men pleasers), knowing that from the Lord you will receive the inheritance, for you serve the Lord Christ. But he who does wrong will be repaid for what he has done, and there is no partiality."[8] Some people have a difficult time with the word "master" because it invokes feelings of losing one's free will. In terms of our relationship with God, it means accepting His will over our will because we know that His will is perfect and our will is, at its best, very flawed. Jesus, our Lord, is the perfect example of what it looks like for a man to accept his role as servant and trust in God as his master. I think we sometimes forget that although Jesus was/is 100% God, while on earth he was also 100% human with a human mind, a human will, and human emotions.

So how do we learn to trust God as our Master and accept our role as His servant? The Apostle Paul put it best when he said: *"For me to live is Christ, and to die is gain. But if I live on in the flesh, this will mean fruit from my labor; yet what I shall choose I cannot tell, having a desire to depart and be with Christ, which is far better."*[9] Paul understood that his purpose on earth was to serve God and spread the Gospel of Jesus Christ to the Gentiles. He knew that his life was not his own, but rather the property of

7   Guralnik, David B. (1982). Webster's New World Dictionary: Second College Edition. New York, NY: Simon & Schuster

8   Colossians 3:23-25, NKJV

9   Philippians 1:21-23, NKJV

11

Consensual Christianity

Christ *(For me to live is Christ)*. Paul also had an understanding of where his reward would come from and when it would come *(and to die is gain)*. The next part of the verse is what I really want to focus on, *(But if I live on in the flesh, this will mean fruit from my labor; yet what I shall choose I cannot tell)*. Paul had a unique and undeniable understanding of his role as the servant of Christ. He understood that his labor and suffering here produced fruit for the Kingdom of God. Paul also understood that he had a choice to either continue his work or to stop serving his Master. Our time here on earth is not about us. Even though we may sometimes suffer and go through hardship, it is all for the Kingdom of God if we live in God's will. God, our Master, has promised us rewards in heaven for the work we do here on earth. We do not labor in vain! Understanding our role as servant gives us a greater understanding of our calling, which will in turn allow us to produce much more fruit for the Kingdom.

As our Master, God does not require us to work our hands to the bone. He simply requires our submission: submission to His will, submission to His sovereignty, and submission to His authority. He is still Jehovah and will provide for all of our needs! Jesus tells us how He, the Master, will treat us, His servants in Matthew 11:28-30: *"Come to Me, all you who labor and are heavy laden, and I will give you rest. Take My yoke upon you and learn from Me, for I am gentle and lowly in heart, and you will find rest for your souls. For My yoke is easy and My burden is light."* The reason that it seems like our burden is so heavy at times, is because we resist, we wrestle with God, and give in to the temptation to get off the path He

12

is leading us down. He promises us rest, a yoke that is easy, and a burden that is light. All of the weight that we feel is not from Him. It is the weight that we have piled on from sin and trying to do for ourselves what only God can do in our lives. Once we accept His yoke, He will lead us and provide all we need to get the job done. Remember, His yoke is easy and His burden is light. That does not mean that our path will be obstacle free, but it does mean that He will be right there with us. God, our Master, is not a master of unwilling slaves but rather a master of willing servants; people who serve because they want to serve, not because they are forced to. He is a teacher of students, one who is willing to take us under His wing and show us the way. Just like Paul, we have a choice. We can choose to follow our own will or we can choose to submit to His will. One path, our path, will lead us to destruction. His perfect path will lead us in righteousness and truth. When we take time to consider all that God has given us, how could we not willingly and joyfully submit to Him?

Our Father

"I am the vine and My Father is the vinedresser. Every branch in Me that does not bear fruit, He takes away; and every branch that bears fruit He prunes, that it may bear more fruit. You are already clean because of the word that I have spoken to you; abide in Me and I in you. As the branch cannot bear fruit of itself, unless it abides in the vine, neither can you, unless you abide in Me. I am the vine, you are the branches. He, who abides in

Consensual Christianity

Me and I in him, bears much fruit; for without me you can do nothing. If anyone does not abide in Me, he is cast out as a branch and is withered; and they gather them and throw them into the fire, and they are burned. If you abide in Me and My words abide in you, you will ask what you desire and it shall be done for you. By this My Father is glorified, that you bear much fruit; so you will be My disciples."[10]

There is nothing more important to a father than the growth of his children. From the time a child comes into the world, the father is focused solely on what the child needs to grow and to develop into a successful, mature adult. We set goals for our children and expect them to live up to certain expectations. We find joy in their first steps and their first words. We expect them to display good character and we discipline them when necessary. Although the discipline is just as hard on the father as it is on the child, we know it is required. As a father of five, I have experienced all of these scenarios. One thing I have learned over time is that mothers, by their very nature, always want their babies to be babies. They are nurturers and enjoy the process of nurturing their children. The older the child gets, the less the mother feels the child needs their nurturing. Fathers, on the other hand, try to find ways to make their children grow up. Fathers push their kids and challenge them, hoping that the challenge will cause them to grow stronger and more independent. Just like earthly fathers, our Heavenly Father is concerned with our growth. He is elated when we are born "again," finds joy in us taking our first steps down the path He is leading us, and takes pride in us when we show our spiritual maturity.

The thing we need to understand as children is that there will be times when we make Him proud and there will also be times when we disappoint Him. He knew that when He chose us. There is nothing that we do that comes as a surprise to God. He knows what is best for us and wants us to have a prosperous and fulfilling life, both for His kingdom and also for ourselves. The prosperity I speak of is not financial, although that can be part of it. I equate prosperity to receiving God's best in life, whether it is relational prosperity, spiritual prosperity, physical health, or various other blessing we are not worthy of in life. Prosperity for prosperity's sake is not our goal. Our goal is to be prosperous as a means to further the Kingdom of God. In other words, we should desire blessings so we may have the means to bless others. God is proud when we act in a way that glorifies and honors Him. He becomes disappointed when we make bad decisions, ignore His Word and commandments, or get off track in life. As a father, I have these same emotions when it comes to my children, but disappointment does not mean that I have stopped loving them or love them any less. There are times when a child disobeys the word of their parents and discipline is the only way to correct the behavior. We don't discipline our kids because we enjoy it. We discipline them because we know that it will save them from unnecessary heartache in the future and help to develop positive characteristics in them. It works the same way with our Heavenly Father: *"For if we would judge*

Consensual Christianity

ourselves, we would not be judged, but when we are judged, we are chastened by the Lord, that we may not be condemned by the world."[11]

Understanding discipline is a big part of understanding God as Our Father. *"And you have forgotten the exhortation which speaks to you as sons: My son, do not despise the chastening of the Lord, nor be discouraged when you are rebuked by Him; for whom the Lord loves, he chastens, and scourges every son whom He receives."*[12] God is love! He disciplines His children because He loves us not because He finds joy in our sorrow. I know that being disciplined by our Father is hard and uncomfortable but understand that it is though discipline that God shapes us, molds us, and shows us how much He loves us. He's building our spiritual character and teaching us valuable spiritual lessons. God utilizes each and every situation in your life as an opportunity to help you develop into the man or woman that He created you to be. Nothing is left to chance; He has a purpose in everything you go through. God uses the very trials that the devil intends for evil to help us grow. God turns the attack of the enemy into an advance for His kingdom. I challenge you to look at your trials as an opportunity to grow and make your Father proud; not as points in your life when God was not there. It encourages me to see that even Jesus had times during His life where His flesh did not want to go through the trials that were before Him. Unlike most of us, His response was always, "not My will Father, but Your will be done." Sometimes it is hard for us to say that because

11   1 Corinthians 11:31-32, NKJV

12   Hebrews 12:5-6, NKJV

16

our flesh does not enjoy hardship but as you continue to grow in your relationship with God, understand that fleshly hardships can reap spiritual rewards if we stay focused on Jesus.

So who is this God we speak of? He is our Creator, our Father, our Master, The Alpha and The Omega, and Jehovah. He is all that we need and the hope of all that we could ever want to be. Take the time to get to know God and don't settle for only knowing about Him. The reason Jesus was able to endure the cross is because He had an understanding of God and the promises of God. *"Therefore we also, since we are surrounded by so great a cloud of witnesses, let us lay aside every weight, and the sin which so easily ensnares us, and let us run with endurance the race that is set before us, looking unto Jesus, the author and finisher of our faith, who for the joy that was set before Him endured the cross, despising the shame, and has sat down at the right hand of the throne of God."*[13]

---

[13]   Hebrews 12:1-2, ESV

Consensual Christianity

2

QUALITY TIME

He who dwells in the secret place of the Most High shall abide under the shadow of the Almighty. I will say of the Lord, He is my refuge and my fortress; my God, in Him I will trust.

Psalm 91:1-2

Consensual Christianity

Every relationship needs quality time. Quality time is a time of intimacy, a time of understanding, and a time of getting to know the person you are spending time with. If you remove quality time from any relationship, the relationship will suffer. I remember when my wife and I started dating. We spent every possible moment together. If we weren't together, we were on the phone talking to one another, sharing our hopes and dreams. We would ride around in my car and talk for hours, just getting to know one another. I truly believe that is one of the reasons our relationship has been able to endure the hardships we have faced. We have always made a commitment to spend time together in any way we can. As much as I wish that we could spend every minute of every day together, we cannot. Well we could, but we would probably be homeless and have a bunch of hungry kids. When life gets hectic, we have to make time for one another. Sometimes that means leaving little notes on the mirror, sending text messages, or short phone calls just to hear her voice. Quality time is the fuel of the relationship.

Our relationship with God works the same way. God wants to be a part of every part of our lives. He doesn't want to be boxed into a few minutes of your day; He wants to share your life with you. For most of us, our time with God stops when we say amen or close our Bible, but that should not be the end. He wants us to talk to Him throughout the day. He wants us to ask His permission when we make big decisions and to share our thoughts and feelings with Him. He wants to have a relationship with you, not a series of recurring appointments with you.

20

Chapter 2

In this chapter we are going to focus on 3 questions: Were you taught to God or brought to God? How do you connect to God? And what is the last thing you did to please God? These three questions will help us better understand why we need quality time, how to spend our quality time, and our motivation for spending time with the Lord.

Were you taught to God or brought to God?

If you confess with your mouth the Lord Jesus and believe in your heart that God raised Him from the dead, you will be saved.[14]

Salvation is an awesome gift. The fact that Jesus, the holy Son of God, freely gave His life as the perfect sacrifice for your sins and for my sins is amazing to me. What an awesome act of love. There is nothing we could ever do to earn salvation or deserve salvation. It truly is a gift. Ephesians 2:8-9 tells us that we are saved by grace through faith, not of ourselves. It is the gift of God, not of works, lest any man should boast. All we have to do is accept His free gift and we are saved. How do we truly accept His gift? In this section, our focus will be on answering this question Biblically. There are some things here that may challenge your understanding of God's word. That is my intent! As you go through this portion of the book, please have your Bible handy and search the Scriptures. Ask the Holy Spirit to give you understanding as you read His Word. Don't just take my

---

14   Romans 10:9, NKJV

Chapter 2

In this chapter we are going to focus on 3 questions: Were you taught to God or brought to God? How do you connect to God? And what is the last thing you did to please God? These three questions will help us better understand why we need quality time, how to spend our quality time, and our motivation for spending time with the Lord.

Were you taught to God or brought to God?

If you confess with your mouth the Lord Jesus and believe in your heart that God raised Him from the dead, you will be saved.[14]

Salvation is an awesome gift. The fact that Jesus, the holy Son of God, freely gave His life as the perfect sacrifice for your sins and for my sins is amazing to me. What an awesome act of love. There is nothing we could ever do to earn salvation or deserve salvation. It truly is a gift. Ephesians 2:8-9 tells us that we are saved by grace through faith, not of ourselves. It is the gift of God, not of works, lest any man should boast. All we have to do is accept His free gift and we are saved. How do we truly accept His gift? In this section, our focus will be on answering this question Biblically. There are some things here that may challenge your understanding of God's word. That is my intent! As you go through this portion of the book, please have your Bible handy and search the Scriptures. Ask the Holy Spirit to give you understanding as you read His Word. Don't just take my

---

14   Romans 10:9, NKJV

21

Consensual Christianity

word for it; search and know the Scriptures for yourself.

When we accept God's gift of salvation, several things happen inside of us. First, we acknowledge that we have reached an intellectual understanding of our need for a Savior. We are also acknowledging that we have an understanding of the Gospel message that Jesus is the only Savior, the only one able to cleanse us of our sins. Secondly, we submit willingly to Christ's Lordship in our lives. Our willing submission, also commonly referred to as submitting of one's own volition, is our acknowledging that we not only know but we also believe that Jesus is the only Way, the Truth, and the Life. Thirdly, the Holy Spirit, who has convicted us of our sins and brought us to the point of repentance, comes to dwell inside of us and seals us for the day of Salvation. He, the Holy Spirit, begins the process of sanctification in our lives. The word *"sanctification"* means to set apart. In simpler terms, the Holy Spirit begins to clean us up. He renews our mind as we spend time in His word. He begins to purge us as He removes the impurities from our life. Lastly, He molds us into what He created and designed us to be.

If we look at all of this in light of Romans 10:9, it is our intellectual understanding of the Gospel and our need for a Savior that leads us to confession. Subsequently, it is the heart held belief that Jesus, through His death, burial, and resurrection, has the power to save which leads to our willing submission to Him as Lord. As it relates to being taught to God or brought to God, it is really a question of where you are in the process. An individual being brought to God is the result of all we have

22

discussed previously. The individual has come to an understanding that they are a sinner (by the conviction of the Holy Spirit) in need of a Savior. This understanding is followed by belief in Christ's power to save and the individual's volitional submission to Him as Lord. The individual's confession that Jesus is Lord is an outward expression of the inward belief that God did indeed raise Jesus from the dead. This individual is saved!

Being taught to God, on the other hand, is purely an intellectual change in that it involves a change of mind, but not a change of heart. I attended several Christian schools throughout the course of my childhood. I also attended church multiple times per week, Christian summer camps, and was part of a vibrant youth ministry. Consequently, I knew God's word very well. Well, at least I knew God's word intellectually. I memorized Bible verses on a regular basis and knew all of the most popular hymns and songs. Before I go on, let me say that I would not trade that experience for anything. God used the things I learned during that time to help me later in life. I will admit, however, that I assumed I was saved at the time because I said and did all of the right things. I had a good amount of intellectual knowledge about God but I was not in relationship with God. I was taught to God.

Please don't get me wrong, I am not suggesting, in any way, that being raised in church, Christian school, or a godly home is bad in any way. My intent is to simply point out that no amount of intellectual understanding about God can save you. James 2:19 is an interesting verse, it states, *"You believe there is one God. You do well. Even the demons believe – and tremble."* I think that James was somewhat sarcastically telling people that simply believing there is a God is not enough to save you. Even the demons believe there is a God and we know where they are headed. 2 Peter 1:10 is the reason for this section in the book. It says, *"Therefore, brethren, be even more diligent to make your call and election sure, for if you do these things you will never stumble."*

This may all seem really deep and heavy, but I am not trying to scare you. Or maybe I am trying to scare you. I would be remiss if I did not challenge you to ensure that your salvation is sure. That is not to say that Christ's power to save is unsure, God forbid! It is to say, however, that some make an emotional response to a good sermon or a moving testimony. Their subsequent prayer is not a prayer of volitional submission; it is a prayer of emotional response or intellectual arousal. You may think I am overstepping my bounds, but the Bible makes it clear that there are people going through the motions who are not truly saved. Matthew 7:21-23 is a frightening reminder that this is true. One thing to keep in mind is, when the Holy Spirit comes to dwell inside of you, you will change. It is impossible to remain the same. The process of change is different for everyone, so don't expect people to fully change immediately, but change is a definite byproduct of salvation. 2 Corinthians 5:17 says if anyone is in Christ, he is a new creature. Old things have passed away and all things have become new.

Being taught, however, does play a major role. Remember, the prayer of willing submission is preceded by an intellectual understanding of the Gospel message. There are several things we must understand on an intellectual level. First, we must understand that we are dead in sin and separated from God. Secondly, we must understand that Jesus died for our sins and to reconcile us to the Father. Thirdly, we must both understand and believe that Jesus rose on the third day, defeating death, hell, and the grave. We must also understand and believe that Jesus is the only way to the Father. So, as you can see, there is an intellectual component to salvation.

The difference between being taught to God and brought to God is the work of the Holy Spirit. The greatest sermon ever preached is powerless to save a person's soul or even change their life without the power of the Holy Spirit working inside of them; convicting them of sin and drawing them to Christ. I love to teach. Teaching others about God and His word is probably my favorite thing to do. I had to learn early on that I cannot teach a person to accept Christ. I am simply a laborer. I plant seeds, and water seeds planted by others. It is God who brings the increase. I don't have the power to draw anyone to Christ. Keep this in mind as you share your faith with others. Present the Gospel in truth, with respect and with love. Don't be discouraged if the person is not ready to accept God's gift of salvation at that moment. Just keep planting seeds and be available when they are ready. You may have the sincere pleasure of being the one to witness their salvation, or someone else may water the seeds you planted and get the honor of witnessing their salvation. The goal is for the person to come to Christ. It is the Holy Spirit's job to convict them of sin and to draw them in.

So, how does this relate to spending quality time with God? Quality time is all about relational intimacy. Sin separates us from God, a separation that can only be bridged by the blood of Jesus. We cannot be in relationship with God if we have not first accepted His gift of salvation. The blood of Jesus justifies us before God. Jesus bore the punishment we deserved to settle our account. He paid the ultimate price for our sins. Our society tends to associate intimacy with sex. It is much more than that. However, if we look at that association, true intimacy between a man and woman can only exist under the covering of marriage. Marriage is a covenant between husband, wife, and God. Likewise, true intimacy with God can only occur when we are in covenant with Him; the covenant sealed by the blood of Jesus Christ. Isaiah 64:6 says that all our righteousness (apart from Christ) are like filthy rags. The best of all that we have and the greatest of all that we can do is like garbage to God. It is only through the righteousness of Jesus, poured out over our lives, that we are able to have quality time with our Heavenly Father.

How do you connect to God?

Now that God has brought you to Himself, how do you connect to Him? What is the way that you share your intimate time with Him? This is something that is critical to our lives as believers. Knowing how you connect to God will help you when you go through periods where you do not "feel" very close to God. It is in these moments of loneliness that we need to connect to God the most. Writing a book like this has really caused me to take a long hard look at myself. I really believe that God has been using this book to minister to me, maybe even more so than using me to minister to you. My primary way of connecting or feeling close to God is through praise and worship. No matter what is going on, no matter how low I feel, God always seems to put a song in my heart and I cannot help but sing it. Everyone is different. Just because my favorite way to connect is through praise and worship that does not mean that you will get the same feeling that I do. Your way of connecting may be through prayer, reading the Bible, ministering to others, spending time observing and admiring God's creation, or by simply being still and listening for His voice. It is very important that you know and understand your favorite method of connecting to God, but it is equally important that you do not focus solely on the one or two ways that come easiest to you. As human beings, we have been designed to experience things in multiple ways and through multiple senses. It is essential that we use all of our senses to enjoy these experiences. It is also essential as Christians that we learn to connect with God in more than one way. Praise and worship is a wonderful thing but what if I did that all the time and never spent time reading the Bible or meditating on God's Word, or praying. I would be a malnourished Christian. That is the equivalent of an athlete trying to be healthy by eating broccoli all of the time. Is broccoli healthy? Sure it is, but your body needs protein and other nutrients that broccoli alone cannot supply.

Consensual Christianity

Let's look at prayer for instance. If you never pray, you never have an opportunity to cast your cares on Him. *"Be anxious for nothing, but in all things, by prayer and supplication with thanksgiving, let your request be made known unto God; and the peace of God, which surpasses all understanding, will guard your hearts and minds through Christ Jesus," (Philippians 4:6-7).* Likewise, if you do not spend time in the Word, you are missing the only offensive piece of the Armor of God that we have. *"And take the helmet of Salvation, and the sword of the Spirit, which is the Word of God."*[15] God does not want us to be one-dimensional, He wants to enjoy us and He wants us to enjoy the fullness of all that He is, in every way that we can.

So, how often do we leave our spirit feeling malnourished? As we grow closer to God, it is imperative that we have balance, not just for ourselves, but also for our fellow believers. We are here to equip and edify one another. There are times when we are with our brothers and sisters in Christ that we will need to pray for one another, share the word with one another, and join together in the worship of our King. Your walk with God is not just about you. Let me repeat that, your walk with God is not just about you. It is about everyone around you; your spouse, your kids, your neighbors, your coworkers, and your fellow Christians. They all count on you to be willing, ready, and able to step up to the plate when necessary.

If you study the history or strategy of war, you will notice that the first the thing to be attacked by one side is the enemy's communications, followed by the supply lines. This is also true in the spiritual war that we fight on a daily basis. The first thing Satan will do is attack our communication with the Father by convincing us that we will never understand the Bible, or that our prayers are not being heard, or that our praise and worship is meaningless. Remember, Satan tries to thwart the plan of God in our lives and one of the means he uses is to cause confusion in our understanding of God's word by causing us to question what God says, i.e., Eve in the Garden of Eden. The truly sad part is that we occasionally believe him. He is the father of lies, yet we choose to accept his word over the word of our Father. Once we accept the gift of salvation, we are given a direct line of communication to Heaven, one that no force on earth or any attack by the devil can destroy. The second thing he will do is attack our supply line. He will work hard to isolate you and keep you from whatever supplies you may need. This is where it is extremely important to know that our help comes from the Lord and that no attack of the devil is powerful enough to change who we are in Christ or the promises of God in our lives. The attacks only have power over us when we allow them to: *"No weapon formed against you shall prosper, and every tongue which rises against you in judgment you shall condemn. This is the heritage of the servants of the Lord, and their righteousness is from Me, says the Lord."*[6]

Why do you connect with God?

The next question I will ask is why do you connect with

16   Isaiah 54:17, NKJV

Consensual Christianity

God? I have asked myself this question before and the answer is not what you may expect. So why do I connect with God? Is it to give Him glory? Does it satisfy some need or void in my life? Is it the "in" thing to do? Or is it because I find purpose when I connect with Him? The truth is that it is normally for some selfish reason. I have often noticed that the lonelier I feel or the tougher my current situation may be, the more I try to connect with God. Let's be real, that is not really connecting with God. That is more like a junkie looking for the next fix; trying to find the one thing that makes reality seem a little less real and life a little more ideal. It is human nature for us to be selfish but that is not what God has called us to. He has called us to be selfless and to place His kingdom, His word, and His calling above all else. Our life's journey, seeking after Him, should be the centerpiece of all that we do. I used to live under the misconception that my life's journey would lead me to God when the truth really is that God is my life's journey. I am not being led to Him, as His child, I am willingly and obediently following Him.

And we know that all things work together for the good of those who love God, to those who are the called according to His purpose. For whom He foreknew, He also predestined to be conformed to the image of His Son, that He might be the firstborn among many brethren. Moreover whom He predestined, these He also called; whom He called, these He also justified; and whom He justified, these He also glorified."[17]

---

17   Romans 8:28-30, NKJV

Chapter 2

The answer to the question, "Why do we connect with God?" should be an easy one: because we want to get to know Him, to spend time in His presence, and because it pleases Him. We were made to commune with our heavenly Father. He is the cure to all of the ills in life, the only one that can fill the voids in our heart. It is hard to maintain a relationship where there is no connection, no communication, and no intimacy. The connection, our connection to the Father is Jesus Christ. The communication we have with Him is our time in prayer and reading His word. Our intimacy with Him is inviting Him into each and every part of our lives; into the good moments and the bad.

What was the last thing you did to please God?

But seek first the kingdom of God and His righteousness, and all these things shall be added to you. Therefore do not worry about tomorrow, for tomorrow will worry about its own things. Sufficient for the day is its own trouble."[8]

Seek ye first the kingdom of God! How often do we actually seek Him first? What was the last thing you did just to make God smile or bring Him joy? I recently asked myself this very question and after much contemplation, the answer startled me. The truth is that I really don't know. The Bible is full of principles like sowing and reaping, giving and receiving, doing

18   Matthew 6:33, NKJV

31

Consensual Christianity

unto others as you would have them do unto you. In the midst of my contemplation, I discovered that I was following these principles for the wrong reasons. I was giving so that I would receive in return and not to please God by bringing glory to Him through my giving. I was sowing, not out of obedience, but in expectation of reaping. As believers, everything we do should be done to bring glory to God, not reward to ourselves. The rewards are supposed to be a bonus for our pleasure because of our obedience. Conversely, they are not intended to be the purpose of our obedience. We should obey God because we love Him and want to bring Him joy, not for selfish gains. So let me ask you a question; do you give to help supply the local church with the tools it needs to fight the good fight, or do you give simply to see what you will get in return? What are the motives behind the things that you do for God?

I know that I need to be cautious as I write this because I do not want to discourage you from expecting or receiving God's blessings. However, I do want to draw your attention to what it is that truly motivates you. I also want to make sure that you understand the difference between purpose and motivation. I believe that God gives us the promise of rewards and blessings so that we can endure the trials that lay before us; but the purpose of those trials is to bring glory to God through our faith and trust in Him as well as the completion of His will for our lives. It is perfectly acceptable and expected for us to be excited about the rewards we will receive as a result of following God's will and commandments. *"Looking unto Jesus, the author and finisher of our*

32

faith, who for the joy that was set before Him endured the cross, despising the shame, and has sat down at the right hand of the throne of God."[19] Jesus knew that the cross was not something that His flesh wanted to go through, but knowing the rewards and the promises of God allowed Him to endure what He had to endure. That was His motivation, but His purpose was completely different. Contrary to popular belief, His purpose was not to bring us salvation; His purpose was to glorify God by affording us the means to get to know God; to develop a relationship with Him. *"Jesus spoke these words, lifted up His eyes to heaven, and said: "Father, the hour has come. Glorify Your Son, that Your Son also may glorify You, as You have given Him authority over all flesh, that He should give eternal life to as many as You have given Him. And this is eternal life, that they may know You, the only true God, and Jesus Christ whom You have sent. I have glorified You on the earth. I have finished the work which You have given Me to do. And now, O Father, glorify Me together with Yourself, with the glory which I had with You before the world was."[20]* Do your actions bring glory to God or do they bring glory to you? Do you do things in public so that others will see or is your focus on the purpose instead of the person, you? *"But when you do a charitable deed, do not let your left hand know what your right hand is doing, that your charitable deed may be in secret; and your Father who sees in secret will Himself reward you openly."[21]* My greatest fear in writing this book is that I would become too excited about seeing my name on the cover. We are

---

19   Hebrews 12:2, NKJV

20   John 17:1-5, NKJV

21   Matthew 6:3-4, NKJV

taught from birth that our successes determine who we are. We consider parents a success if their kids go to college, don't get in any legal trouble, wait until they are married before they have any kids, and are upstanding citizens. We consider others successful based on their income, title or position, house size and car brand. That is not how God determines our success rate. We have a natural inclination to love attention and the feeling of being wanted or needed. Sometimes, we allow the attention to make us feel like we are more than we truly are. *"Do not be deceived, my beloved brethren. Every good gift and every perfect gift is from above, and comes down from the Father of lights, with whom there is no variation or shadow of turning."*[22] Everything that we have, everything that we achieve, everything that we are given comes from God. Without God we are nothing nor can we do anything. He made us who we are and we are here for His purpose. Whatever gifts and talents you possess have come from God, so whatever material or monetary gain you obtain as a result of those gifts and talents are from Him as well. It is important to keep that perspective as believers, so that the messenger never becomes more important than the message. We are here to share God with the world, through whatever medium we are gifted and everything that we do should bring glory to God through Jesus Christ our Lord.

What's your focus?

When I think about quality time, I think about time spent with my wife and kids. Quality time for us is sitting around

---

[22]   James 1:16-17, NKJV

the dinner table talking about our day, going to the park, going swimming, going out to dinner or the movies, or just going for a drive and listening to music. Quality time is all about being together, not just physically, but also spiritually, mentally, and emotionally. Quality time with God is no different. It is all about being with Him spiritually, mentally, physically, and emotionally. You may be thinking, "I know how to be with God spiritually, but how can I be with Him mentally, physically, and emotionally?" Well, God designed us to experience things in various ways. Think about eating your favorite food. The primary way you interact with that food is through your sense of taste, but don't you also enjoy the smell of the food, and the way it looks on your plate. In some cases, like me and fajitas, you can also enjoy the way the food sounds as it sizzles in the pan. Now, smelling or hearing the food will not quench your hunger the way eating the food will, but that does not mean that your sense of smell or sense of hearing are not involved in the overall experience.

Experiencing God mentally, as well as physically, is all about your focus. One thing I often struggle with during my quality time with the Lord is keeping my mind from wandering. I know I am not the only one. Consequently, I have had to experiment with the ways in which I spend quality time with the Lord to find what works best for me. I've found that it is easier for me to focus mentally early in the morning, so I usually read my Bible as soon as I wake up. My brain usually feels like a blank slate at that point so there is not a bunch of junk cluttering my thoughts. I have also discovered that it is easier for me to pray while listening to worship music. The music acts as a mental buffer for me while I am quietly sitting and listening for His voice. We are all different, so the ways in which we spend quality time will be different as well.

One last thought: God is more concerned with quality than quantity. If you are the type of person who can truly pray for hours, that is great, but if you are more like me, and pray for much shorter periods, that is fine as well. God is not keeping a log of how long you pray or how many chapters you read. Some of the most profound revelations I have received from God's Word came after reading just a few verses. If you have committed to read 15 chapters a day, that is great. Just know that God will not be disappointed if you only read 15 verses, He is after your heart, and therefore more concerned with your attitude and intentions. Praying for 2 hours just so you can say you prayed for 2 hours is a waste of 2 hours because your heart is in the wrong place. The Bible tells us of the importance of spending continual time with God throughout the day. Psalm 1 tells us that the man who meditates on God's law day and night is blessed. The Apostle Paul tells us, in I Thessalonians 5, to pray without ceasing. God should be a constant, consistent part of our daily lives. It is good to set aside daily time to study God's word and pray, but we should not confine God to that particular time slot. Our relationship with God should permeate every area of our life.

God is more interested in the quality of your time with

Him than the quantity. Don't allow the devil to convince you that you are less of a Christian if you do not spend as much time in prayer or reading your Bible as someone else. That may seem contradictory to my statement about our relationship with God permeating every area of our life, but I am specifically speaking about time that we set aside for the purpose of daily prayer and study, devotion time.

In reality, we need both, intentional and purposeful devotion time where we block everything else out so we can focus on Him, and we need to ensure that He is a part of every area of our daily life. Be consistent, be deliberate, and be authentic. God can give you 5 hours of revelation in 5 minutes if you are in tune with His heart and listening to His voice.

Consensual Christianity

3

Trusting God in the Quiet Times

"Why are you so cast down, O my soul? And why are you disquieted within me? Hope in God, for I shall yet praise Him for the help of His countenance.

Psalm 42:5

Consensual Christianity

Of all the chapters in this book, this is the one that I have spent the most time learning throughout the course of my relationship journey. I grew up in a broken home; my mother and father were never married. I can count on one hand the number of times I saw my father while I was a child. One of the side effects of that broken relationship is difficulty in establishing relationships with males, especially those in positions of authority. Now, my educational background is in psychology so I could probably provide you with a few textbook reasons why I struggle in that area but I think you get the point. As a teen, I really struggled with this, that is, until four men entered my life and took the time to develop relationships with me that taught me how to trust men. Every man in my life, up until that point, had hurt me either physically or emotionally.

I didn't allow men to get close to me because I assumed that they would just leave or not be there when I needed them. I can't help but laugh when I look back because I tried so hard to push these guys away, but they would not give up on me. These men taught me how to be a husband, a father, a man, and a friend. I would not be where I am today if not for them. In fact, I would be remiss if I did not say thank you Jim, Ron, Bruce, and Kevin. Thank you for allowing God to love me and train me through you, and for being practical examples of strong, godly men for me. As a kid with trust issues, it was difficult for me to learn to trust God. I just assumed He would either hurt me in some way or just disappear like all of the others. Notice that I said I had to learn to trust God. It was not an overnight thing, but it was definitely necessary. If you think back to chapter one, one of the five aspects of God we discussed is His role as our Father. Some of you may be like me: You struggle to trust God in that area because you could not trust your earthly father. Believe me when I tell you, God is faithful and trustworthy. You don't have to worry about Him leaving you or letting you down.

As believers, we have our peaks and our valleys, our highs and our lows. In the midst of the highs we often experience joy, peace, and trust. In the midst of the lows, we learn to rely on God more and more every day. We often experience anger with the enemy for the attack that we are under and try to find ways to praise our way through while God brings us to victory. But what do we do during those times when we feel nothing? You know what I am talking about, the time that you don't feel that closeness to God that you love so much. You find yourself saying, "Hello God, I'm still here," and you hear nothing in return. You read your Bible and you pray; you sing songs of praise and worship, but you feel like your words are meaningless, falling on deaf ears. These are the times that will test the most secure Christians; the days when you feel like your relationship is going nowhere. Well, know this, as a Christian, whether you feel it or not, your relationship is always going somewhere. The true question is whether you are progressing or regressing. There are two words that we are going to focus on in this section; two words that will define your life as a believer: faith and trust. My belief is that these two words hold the key to the quiet times we experience in our walk with the Lord.

Faith & Trust

Why do so many people say "no" to God's gift of salvation? Why do so many people turn their back on Christ? In my opinion, it has very little to do with the act of accepting Christ as Savior; it has much more to do with the requirement to accept Him as Lord. Who in their right mind would turn down an eternity in Heaven in exchange for a trip to hell? It is hard to trust a God that you cannot see. We use words like "faith" and "trust" when we talk about relating to God, words that are difficult to grasp just based on our human understanding. Faith and trust are words that require us to step outside of our free will and to step outside of our comfort zone. It is easy to say you have faith about your finances when you have an excessive amount of money; the excess is tangible. However, the opposite scenario is rather difficult; when your outgo is more than your income. How do you have faith in the midst of that storm? What do you do? God allows our faith to be challenged. He constantly asks for our trust; He requires it; even to the point of salvation. *"For there is no difference; for all have sinned and fall short of the glory of God, being justified freely by His grace through the redemption that is in Christ Jesus, whom God set forth as a propitiation by His blood, through faith, to demonstrate His righteousness, because in His forbearance God had passed over the sins that were previously committed, to demonstrate at the present time His righteousness, that He might be just and the justifier of the one who has faith in Jesus."*[23] So, what do you do when you are unsure? Well, what did Jesus do? He did what was required of

[23]   Romans 3:22-26, NKJV

Him, even unto death. Jesus Christ has been where you are. He understands. It is in Him that we place our faith, but even more importantly, it is Him who gives us our faith. *"Therefore, since we are surrounded by so great a cloud of witnesses, let us also lay aside every weight, and sin which clings so closely, and let us run with endurance the race that is set before us, looking to Jesus, the founder and perfecter of our faith, who for the joy that was set before Him endured the cross, despising the shame, and is seated at the right hand of the throne of God.*[24] So we do exactly what He did, we trust and we have faith. We believe in the promises of God and use them as motivation to help us fulfill the call of God on our lives and ultimately bring glory to the Father. Jesus is the ultimate example of bringing God glory by putting aside His flesh and having faith beyond His comfort zone. As Christians we are to be Christ-like; how much more Christ-like can we be than surrendering our flesh for God's greater purpose?

So what do we do to get out of the rut that we have so easily slipped into? The answer lies in the way that you respond to the situation. Will you respond spiritually, with the mind of Christ, or will you respond carnally, allowing your mind and your emotions to run rampant? Our fleshly actions are an indication of our spiritual growth. As spiritual babies, we may react to trials and tribulations much like a natural baby would react to an unpleasant situation. We may cry, kick and scream, and throw a temper tantrum, but this is only because we do not know how to react. The further along we get in our walk with God, the more

[24]   Hebrews 12:1-2, ESV

our reactions should reflect His actions. The more we mature, the more we should become like our Father. God will never allow us to be tempted beyond what we can handle. Likewise, He will never allow us to go through a

trial where He is not there by our side. He promises to never leave us or forsake us; yet, we often respond to situations like spoiled little brats. What if Jesus walked away from the Cross, simply because it seemed too hard to endure? What if He would have allowed His faith to be shaken or His trust in God to waiver? What if He allowed His circumstances to become His focus instead of focusing on the will of the Father? These may seem like trivial questions to you, but the truth is that at any point in time Jesus could have backed down. When He was born of the Virgin Mary, He became a man and just like a man He had a free will. Jesus was not a robot. He was not a puppet with strings that reached up to heaven being controlled by the Father. So what if He walked away the way that we so often do? What hope would there be for the world? Where would you and I be today? That is a situation that I am glad I do not have to live in. I am thankful that Jesus had enough faith in God's purpose and trust in God's promises to endure the cross.

The real question is how do we approach our "cross?" Do we walk away because of fear or do we endure it because of faith? In my life, there have been plenty of times that I have walked away because of my circumstances. I know that life can be difficult and the calling of God can test even the most seasoned Christians, but I also know that God is love and love never fails. As believers, we have become so comfortable with the status quo. We act as though we are doing our part by going to church, listening to Christian music, and putting our kids in Christian school. The bottom line is that a lot of us have missed it. We have totally and completely missed it. We have become complacent. We have placed all of our focus on God's promises and lost sight of His purpose. The time has come for us to shed all of the unnecessary baggage that we have picked up along the way and focus on the calling that God has given us. We are here to bring God glory through faith in His Son, trust in His Word, and an unwavering commitment to complete His mission. Are you doing that or have your circumstances become god in your life? I truly believe that the quiet times we experience happen because we have allowed circumstances to interfere with our relationship with God. We allow Satan to convince us that God doesn't want to be bothered right now. We allow doubt to creep in and dilute our faith. We allow fear to come in and our trust in God starts to change into trust in our own ability to change the situation or lack thereof. Doubt and fear are the enemies of faith and trust. *"Trust in the Lord with all your heart, and lean not on your own understanding; in all your ways acknowledge Him, and He shall direct your paths. Do not be wise in your own eyes; fear the Lord and depart from evil. It will be health to your flesh, and strength to your bones."*[25]

So where do we begin this journey of trust? Our first step in the journey is trusting that Jesus is indeed the Messiah,

[25] Proverbs 3:5-8, NKJV

45

Consensual Christianity

the Son of God made flesh; that He died as the perfect sacrifice for our imperfect lives, and in His resurrection, the keys to death, hell, and the grave were stripped away from Satan. One of the most difficult areas in which we need to exercise trust is the area of forgiveness. We often feel that our sins are too big to be forgiven and that God never accounted for our sins when He sent Jesus to die for them. The Blood of Jesus is not type specific; it covers all sin. Jesus did not die to bring forgiveness for only certain sins. He died to bring forgiveness for all sins! God knows about everything that you have done and will do. Believe in the fact that Jesus died for all of those sins. Feeling that our sins are too big or bad for God is a tactic the devil uses to dilute our trust in God. Never lose your trust in God! There is nothing that you could do to make Him stop loving you. God is love. *"Love suffers long and is kind; love does not envy; love does not parade itself, is not puffed up; does not behave rudely, does not seek its own, is not provoked, thinks no evil; does not rejoice in iniquity, but rejoices in the truth; bears all things, believes all things, hopes all things, endures all things; love never fails."*[26] This is God's description of Himself. *"He who does not love does not know God, for God is love."*[27] The truth is that to truly trust God, you must first know His love. As humans we don't just give trust away; it is developed over time and through a process. Understanding God's love is a giant step in that process. Most of us don't have any trouble trusting our mother's love; it is a natural thing. The reason it seems natural is because

---

26   1 Corinthians 13:4-8, NKJV

27   1 John 4:8, NKJV

of the bond that is developed in the womb which continues on from the time we enter the world until the day we are old enough to live on our own. We learn to rely on our mother for nourishment, encouragement, stability, love and guidance. Now, think about the child who grew up without their mother. What type of trust will that child have in their mother? My guess would be little to none simply because the child was never able to experience the things that would cause its level of trust to grow. I said all of that to get to this point: trusting God is a process. If you are living your life with little or no trust in God, it is simply because you have not given God the opportunity to earn your trust. You have not given Him the opportunity to provide you with nourishment, encouragement, stability, love, and guidance. In order for your trust to grow, you have to give a little bit of it away.

I love to read the book of Psalms; I marvel at the way David trusted in God, and how he knew that, even though he made mistakes, God would always be true to His promises. *"I will love you, O Lord my strength. The Lord is my rock and my fortress and my deliverer; My God, my strength, in whom I will trust; My shield and the horn of my salvation, my stronghold. I will call upon the Lord, who is worthy to be praised; so shall I be saved from my enemies."*[28] What peace David must have had in knowing that he could trust in God. In order for David's trust in God to grow to the point that we see here, he had to give a little trust. I wonder what his life would have turned into had he not stood before Goliath or believed

---

Consensual Christianity

that he was to be king.

Jesus gives us another wonderful example of the benefits of trust. One of the primary benefits of trusting God is peace. Mark 4:35-41 tells us the story of Jesus and the disciples crossing the sea during a great storm. The boat was tossed to and fro by the waves and the disciples were all fearful. They thought they were going to die. Yet verse thirty-eight tells us that Jesus was in the stern of the boat asleep on a pillow. How could He sleep at such a perilous time? I can only imagine what the disciples must have thought: "Here we are, about to die on this sea and Jesus is asleep." Why was He able to sleep? His trust and faith in His heavenly Father gave Him peace that surpassed all understanding. Jesus knew the Father and He knew the Father's purpose for Him. He knew that purpose had not been fulfilled and, as long as He was in the Father's will, He could not die until His appointed time. The speed bumps and roadblocks could not shake or deter Him because He knew His destination and trusted His Father to ensure His arrival. I am not talking about His destination on the other side of the sea but rather His destination in life. He knew His God designed, predestined destination and nothing could deter or discourage Him. How did He develop this great trust and faith? He spent time with His heavenly Father. He prayed and listened to the Father's voice. He trusted the Father's words and had faith in the Father's promises. It is not enough to simply listen to God. We need to also trust that what He says is the absolute truth. Trust is what turns the word that God spoke to you into the work that God does to you and through you.

Faith and trust are our spiritual muscles. The more we exercise them the stronger they become; the more we use them, the more efficient and proficient we become.

So how do we trust God in the quiet times? By faith! Faith is the key to trusting God. We tend to go the wrong way by allowing our feelings to overpower our faith. Just remember that feelings can only detect physical occurrences and although our lives are manifested in the physical they are lived in the spiritual. I want to challenge you, remove the word "feeling" from your vocabulary. Replace the thought or significance of feelings with the principles of faith and trust. Know that God has promised to never leave you or forsake you and that His word is truth. *"Now faith is the substance of things hoped for, the evidence of things not seen. For by it the elders obtained a good testimony. By faith we understand that the worlds were framed by the word of God, so that the things which are seen were not made of things which are visible," (Hebrews 11:1-3).* [29]

Difficult but Necessary:

Faith and trust are difficult to comprehend and possibly even more difficult to apply to our lives because we are so driven by experience and instinct. In some ways we have to erase years of hurt to be able to learn to trust God the way we should. Romans 12:2 says, *"Do not be conformed to this world, but be transformed by the renewing of your mind, that you may prove what is that good and acceptable and perfect will of God."* There is a mental renewing process that all believers must go through. This Scripture in

[29]   Hebrews 11:1-3, NKJV

particular deals with that process as it relates to the world's view of what is right and acceptable, but I believe a big part of that renewing process is learning to trust God and to believe in His promises in spite of your circumstances. In our human minds we can only comprehend that which is humanly possible. Mary, the mother of Jesus, experienced this when the angel appeared to her and told her she would be the mother of the Savior of the world. Mary was troubled because she could not humanly understand how this would be possible. The angel simply said to her, "For with God nothing shall be impossible." Our finite minds will never be able to comprehend God's power but we need to stand firm on the statement that with God nothing shall be impossible.

What does that mean? God has a plan for each and everyone one of His children, and even those who are not His children. God's plan will come to pass. We just have to trust in His word and rest in His sovereignty. God may allow some things to happen in your life, things you do not enjoy. Trust in His plan and His sovereignty. God sees things from an eternal perspective and there are times where our earthly conditions may seem dire to us, but to Him they are not so serious. That does not mean that He does not care about us. It is actually quite the contrary. He cares so much about us that He gives us room to grow. He provides for our needs and keeps us in His loving arms. He sees the whole picture and acts accordingly. We only see small pieces of the picture so we cannot fully understand His plan and His actions.

Lastly, I leave you with the words of Proverbs 3:5-6: *"Trust in the Lord with ALL of your heart and lean not on your own understanding. In ALL of your ways acknowledge Him and He shall direct your paths."* As you read this passage of Scripture, pay attention to the roles listed. Our role is to trust and to acknowledge Him; His role is to direct our path. Being in God's will is trusting Him and acknowledging Him in ALL you do, allowing Him to direct your path. It all starts with trust!

Consensual Christianity

4

Planning for the Future

My son, do not forget my law, but let your heart keep my commands; for length of days and long life and peace they will add to you.

Proverbs 3:1-2

Consensual Christianity

Last summer we took a family trip to Florida. We began planning and saving months in advance. We were all filled with excitement, especially our kids, because it was our first real family vacation. There were a few things we knew in advance. We knew where we were going, we knew how long we were going to be there, we knew what things we wanted to do while we were there, and we knew our budget for the trip. There were also some things we did not know for sure before we left. For instance, when we booked our trip we did not know that it was going to rain every day that we were there. The weather drastically changed our plans, but we did not allow it to ruin our trip. Anyone who has ever planned anything knows that you should always expect the unexpected.

In the end, we were able to do all of the major things we wanted to do, and I think we ultimately had a better time following our altered plan than we would have with our original plan. Unexpected circumstances will arise. When they do, we have to decide if we are going to keep moving forward or tuck our tails and turn back. We could have allowed ourselves to become disappointed and frustrated by the weather but instead we decided to work around it. We have to be flexible and trust that God is in control. Things may not always go according to our plan but nothing catches God off guard. He has a plan and His plan is perfect. He will use the obstacles in your life to help you grow. He will also use them for His glory. Your testimony of power to save and deliver will bring Him glory and help you minister to those going through similar circumstances. The

Chapter 4

Apostle Peter knew this and wrote words of encouragement for you and for me.

"Be sober, be vigilant; because your adversary the devil walks about like a roaring lion, seeking whom he may devour. Resist him, steadfast in the faith, knowing that the same sufferings are experienced by your brotherhood in the world. But may the God of all grace, who called us to His eternal glory by Christ Jesus, after you have suffered a while, perfect, establish, strengthen, and settle you."[30]

Planning for the future is something most mature people would say they do on a continual basis. Whether it is saving to buy your dream home or put your kids through college, or planning for your retirement, we all practice planning for the future in some way. Regardless of the goal, all good plans have a couple things in common. First, they all have a sound blueprint; a plan that actually incorporates all of the necessary steps for success. Secondly, they all have an understanding that we are currently not in the place we ultimately want to be. The majority of this book is written to address the first commonality, the sound blueprint for success. This chapter really focuses on the second commonality, understanding where we are and figuring out how to get to where we want to be.

We will begin by discussing God's blueprint for our lives. Understanding His blueprint for our lives will help us understand where we are and the place we are trying to get to. We will then discuss living in God's presence and the importance

30   1 Peter 5:8-10, NKJV

55

of our conversations with Him. God's presence is our place of refuge and rest on this journey. Our conversations with Him will help us determine our steps along the way. As you read this chapter, take the time to think about and even write down where you believe you are, where you believe your journey is ultimately leading, and the ways in which you can enjoy the trip along the way. We are going to start by looking at part of a very significant Biblical journey, the children of Israel's journey through the wilderness on their way from Egypt to the Promised Land, and some instructions God gave them along the way.

Does your temple match God's blueprint?

Did you know that you are the temple of the Living God? The Holy Spirit dwells inside of you. Take a moment and let that sink in. How amazing is that. To know that no matter where you are, night or day, God is with you. I don't know about you, but that gives me great joy and brings me tremendous comfort. But what does that really mean for you and me? Well, it means a few things. First, you and I are sealed for the day of salvation. That means that the Holy Spirit is our proof that we are God's children. The blood of Jesus cleanses us from sin. It is His blood that paid the price for our freedom and reconciliation to the Father, but it is the Holy Spirit that is the proof of our purchase. The Apostle Paul says it this way in 2 Corinthians 1:21-22: *"Now He who establishes us with you in Christ and has anointed us is God, who also has sealed us and given us the Spirit in our hearts as a guarantee."*

Secondly, you and I are being sanctified daily by the

Holy Spirit as He works in us and through us. Sanctification is the process whereby we become more like Christ. It is the Holy Spirit working in us to remove those things that do not belong; bad habits, addictions, ungodly thoughts and actions, etc. Sanctification is a process and it takes time. In fact, it begins the day we are born again and continues until the day we die. 2 Thessalonians 3:2 says, *"But we are bound to give thanks to God always for you, brethren beloved by the Lord, because God from the beginning chose you for salvation through sanctification by the Spirit and belief in the truth."* As unbelievers, we were driven by our flesh to pursue the lusts or desires of the flesh. As Christians, our pursuits change. We are to seek God's kingdom first, and His righteousness. We are to live a life that pleases Him and not one of self-pleasure. Sanctification is a part of what makes this possible. I list it as a part because there are some other significant things that help us live lives that are pleasing to God. For example, God gives us grace to overcome temptation and makes a way of escape so we can bear it (1 Corinthians 10:13). Apart from His grace to overcome, His strength to endure, and the work of the Holy Spirit in our lives, we would be powerless to stand against temptation and the desires of the flesh. As a last point on sanctification, the Holy Spirit is constantly molding us into what He needs us to be. One of my favorite passages of Scripture illustrates this: *"Coming to Him as to a living stone, rejected by men, but chosen by God and precious, you also, as living stones, are being built up a spiritual house, a holy priesthood, to offer up spiritual sacrifices acceptable to God through Jesus*

Consensual Christianity

Christ.[31]

Thirdly, the Holy Spirit gives us the power and ability to be witnesses for Jesus Christ. Acts 1:8 says, *"But you shall receive power when the Holy Spirit has come upon you, and you shall be witnesses to Me in Jerusalem, and in all Judea and Samaria, and to the end of the earth."* The Holy Spirit is also known as the Spirit of Truth because He leads us and guides us in all truth. The only way we can have any understanding of God is through the Holy Spirit. He opens our spiritual eyes so we can understand His word. He gives us insight so we can minister to those around us and share the Gospel of Jesus Christ. And it is He, the Holy Spirit, who works through us to heal broken hearts, minister to the sick, and bring restoration to the broken.

So, back to the original question, did you know that you are the temple of the Living God? In the Old Testament, God gave Moses very specific details about the design of His tabernacle (Exodus 25). The tabernacle was a mobile, temporary place where God dwelt while the Israelites journeyed from Egypt to the Promised Land. Later in the Old Testament, God gave King David instructions for building His temple in Jerusalem (1 Chronicles 28-29). In both of these instances, God was very specific about what could and could not be in His temple. We are God's mobile, temporary dwelling place on earth until we get to dwell with Him in eternity. God also gives us some specific details about the things we should and should not allow in His temple. For instance, Ephesians 5:3 says, *"But fornication and all uncleanness*

---

31   1 Peter 2:4-5, NKJV

or covetousness, let it not even be named among you, as is fitting for saints; neither filthiness, nor foolish talking, nor course jesting, which are not fitting but rather giving of thanks." There are examples, all throughout the New Testament, of the things that Christians should practice, think on, and participate in. There are also numerous examples of things we are to avoid. We are going to make mistakes, we are going to slip up at times, and we are going to sin. However, sin should not be the norm in our lives. Remember what 1 Peter 2:5 tells us, *"we are being built up a spiritual house, a holy priesthood, to offer up spiritual sacrifices acceptable to God through Jesus Christ."* We are the temple of God and the Holy Spirit is the master builder, crafting us as only He can.

The next question I want you to think about is, "How do we live as the temple of God?" There is one passage of Scripture I want you to remember: 1 Peter 1:15, *"But as He who called you is holy, you also be holy in all your conduct, because it is written, 'Be holy, for I am holy'."* When Peter stated, "it is written," was quoting Leviticus 11:44 which states, *"For I am the LORD your God. You shall therefore consecrate yourselves, and you shall be holy for I am holy."* Being holy is how we live as the temple of God. This may seem like a daunting task, and truthfully it is impossible if we try to do it in and of ourselves. However, the blood of Jesus has already made you and me holy. If you are saved, when God looks at you He sees the righteousness of Christ. Since we are already spiritually holy because of the blood of Christ, our responsibility is to live a holy life. The word "holy" simply means set apart for a specific purpose. We need to live as though God has set us apart for His

Consensual Christianity

own purpose. 1 Corinthians 6:20 says, *"For you were bought at a price; therefore glorify God in your body, and in your spirit which is God's.* The price you and I were bought at is the priceless, precious blood of Jesus. Since we were bought, we now belong to God. The word "therefore" can be rephrased as "As a result or consequently." Jesus paid the price for our freedom from the bondage of sin and its subsequent death. As a result of Jesus paying the price, we now belong to God. Since we belong to God we should glorify Him and honor Him in our bodies, in our thoughts, and in our spirit. We do this by submitting to His will and allowing Him to be in control. His strength is perfected in our weakness so we do not have to do it on our own. We live as the temple of God by glorifying Him in our body and in our spirit, relying on His strength and power, not our own.

Lastly, we often treat the church building as a holy place, but the church building is truly just a building. We as believers are the holy dwelling place because God, the Holy Spirit, dwells in us, not in a man-made building. We should respect the church building but understand that the building is just a building. When you look at yourself, do you see God's temple? I don't mean that to sound vain in any way. I just want you to see yourself the way God sees you. He sees you as the righteousness of Christ, as the temple of His Holy Spirit, and as a royal priesthood. Always remember, you are costly and valuable, purchased with the precious blood of Jesus, and you are being built up a spiritual house, crafted by the Holy Spirit. You are the temple of the Living God, set apart for His own special purpose, therefore glorify and honor Him in your body and your spirit.

Living in God's Presence

A couple of years ago, I was asked to speak at a men's breakfast at a church in my area. It was an awesome privilege, to have the opportunity to share God's word with a room full of men who desired to know Him more. The pastor who organized the breakfast told me the theme for the event was "Growing the God in Me!" He knew my passion for discipleship so he felt I would be a good fit for their theme. At first glance, that seems like a good theme, right? I thought so too. As I was preparing my message though, the Holy Spirit began to lead me in a direction that seemed to contradict their theme. I was a little worried at first until I realized what the Holy Spirit was doing. Jesus referred to the Holy Spirit as the Spirit of Truth and said that He (the Holy Spirit) would lead us and guide us in all truth. We have to be sensitive to His leading. He was leading me and guiding me in the truth, correcting my faulty understanding of His Word. Finally, the day arrived and I was ready to share the message the Holy Spirit had given me. The main point of the message was that our vision was backwards. The men gathered in the church that morning expecting to get a larger dose of God in their lives, but that is not how it works. The real truth, I shared with them, is that we cannot grow God in us, it is us who grow in God. The Bible doesn't say that God gives us a portion of His Holy Spirit when we trust Christ, it says that the same Spirit that raised Jesus from the dead now dwells in us and quickens (makes alive and vibrant) our mortal bodies.[32] I explained to them that our outlook was wrong. We were under the impression that there was some way we could gain greater access to God. What we had to learn to do was give God greater access to us.

This understanding changed my life because, prior to preparing for that meeting, I too thought there was a way I could "get more of God." I came to realize that God had given me all of Him in Jesus; I had to in turn give Him all of me. That feeling that we get during praise and worship, the one we refer to as the presence of God, happens because we usually only have moments of complete surrender to God during times of worship. Worship is when we find it easiest to focus solely on Him and block all of the nonsense and circumstances of life out for a moment. That is when we allow ourselves to be open, vulnerable, and exposed to Him so He can begin to mend our brokenness. Living in God's presence is not a life where I have full access to Him. He gave me full access through Jesus when I accepted His gift of Salvation. Living in God's presence is living a life where He has full access to me! It is a life of full surrender, where all of my sins and hidden places are exposed so they can be dealt with. It is a life of full reliance where I know that He is truly all that I need. It is a life of full submission to His will, His plan, and His purpose, not my own. Living in God's presence is living a life in which I am being led by His Spirit.

Living in God's presence, as many of us define it, is about seeing miracles or the Gifts of the Spirit in action. While

---

[32]   Romans 8:11

those things can have a powerful impact on our lives, we should not pursue them. In fact, Jesus often chastised those who were in pursuit of miracles. We should instead pursue God's word and let it abide in us. We should seek His kingdom first, above all else. We should live lives of complete and total surrender to Him. We have confused demonstrations of the power of God with manifestations of the presence of God. You can live in the presence of God. The question is, are you willing to do what it takes to make that happen? It is easier for us to believe that we can somehow gain greater access to God because that means that we have to simply get God to stop blocking us...it makes Him the responsible party. If that were true, then we don't have more of Him because he doesn't want to give us more and that, at its core, is His fault. However, when we realize that we are the issue, that it is us who have not given Him full access, now the responsibility is ours and we have to do something about it. The good news is that we can trust God with the good and bad parts of our lives. We don't have to be afraid of being open and vulnerable, completely surrendered to Him, and submitted to His will. We do not have a High Priest who cannot sympathize with our weakness. Jesus gives us access to come boldly to the throne of grace to find help in time of need.

There are times when we may experience God in a more tangible way and those times are amazing. I remember one church service in particular when I was a teen. As I mentioned before, I grew up in a fatherless home and had no real idea of what it meant to be loved by a father, or any male figure for that matter, or how to love one back. In this particular service, my youth pastor was preaching about God's love and he made the statement, "Some of you have never experienced God's love. God is your heavenly Father and He loves you dearly." He went on to say, "Some of you do not know what it feels like to be loved by a father because your father has been absent in your life. God wants you to know and feel His love!" My youth pastor then asked those of us from broken homes to stand up because he wanted to pray specifically for us. I was embarrassed but I stood up. As he began to pray, I closed my eyes and I could feel God's love. It was as though He was standing there, hugging me. That may sound crazy to some of you, but it was real to me. Some of you can definitely relate to what I am describing.

That was such a powerful moment for me. It was life changing and heart mending. God demonstrated His power to heal and restore me personally. That moment was the beginning of a process for me, a process of healing. Our relationship with God may have moments like that. Those moments, when they occur, should be cherished. They should not, however, be the focus of our relationship. In other words, we should not assume that God is not there or concerned with us when we do not feel Him the way we do in those special moments. We need to understand that God is always with us, whether we feel Him or not. It has been my experience that God allows those tangible moments when they are really needed, like a fatherless child needing to feel a father's love in a tangible way. God has promised to never leave you nor forsake you; He is always with you!

Living in God's presence comes with what some may perceive as risks. When we live lives of total and complete submission to God, it moves us outside of our normal comfort zone. We can often find ourselves in a place that is unfamiliar to our human emotions and our human psyche, a place where we feel we have lost control. Now, hear me clearly on this, you have not lost control. Quite the contrary actually, you have given control of your life to God. Picture this scenario with me for a moment; I am driving around a high mountain, navigating a narrow road. I should tell you that I have been driving since long before it was legal for me to drive (I grew up in the country), so I am pretty comfortable behind the steering wheel. I am a good drive but I have never driven in the mountains. In that scenario, wouldn't it be best for me to allow a driver with experience navigating the terrain to take control of the vehicle?

Well, God is the most qualified one to navigate your life. He knows all of the obstacles you will face and the best path to take to get you to His predetermined destination. Still, some consider it risky to give God full control and I believe the reason they feel that way lies in one of three areas: (1) they are afraid of being called. They are afraid that God will call them to preach or to the mission field and they have no desire to do anything like that. (2) They are afraid of being called out. They fear being exposed because they feel that all of their sins and deepest, darkest secrets will be revealed. (3) They are afraid they may experience Him once but never again. This fear goes back to the pursuit of feeling God's presence that we discussed previously. As we move forward, we will discuss these three areas in greater detail.

Afraid of being called. When you spend time in the presence of God, He reveals His will to you. It was in God's presence, at the burning bush, that God told Moses how He would use Moses to lead Israel out of captivity. Knowing that we could be called out of our comfort zone can be a fearful thing. It is natural for humans to pursue comfort, so it goes against our very nature in a sense. Moses could have responded, "Lord, I can't go back to Egypt, they will kill me. I have a wife and a house now and we are happy and settled," but he didn't. Sometimes, God will ask us to go a different direction but often times He wants to use us right where we are. The fact of the matter is that being outside of the will of God is the most dangerous and uncomfortable place you could ever be. Better to leave your comfort for Him than to lose your comfort forever because of you. God is the same yesterday, today, and forever; He is moving in the same direction He always has, we are the ones who change course.

Afraid of being called out. The perfect example of this is in Genesis 3:8, *"And they heard the sound of the Lord walking in the garden in the cool of the day, and Adam and his wife hid themselves from the presence of the Lord God among the trees of the garden. Then the Lord God called to Adam and said to him, 'where are you?' So he said, 'I heard your voice in the garden and I was afraid because I was naked and I hid myself.'*

Adam hid because he had sinned and his sin caused him to be ashamed. I believe that the shame we feel because of sin keeps us out of the presence of God more than the sin itself. Why should we feel ashamed, God knows that we sin; Romans 3:23 says that all have sinned and fallen short of the glory of God. We don't have to be ashamed. The Bible says that when Jesus died on the cross and was raised from the dead He despised the shame. The Bible tells us clearly our position on shame and condemnation. *"Therefore, there is no condemnation for those who are in Christ Jesus, who do not walk according to the flesh but according to the Spirit. For the law of the spirit of life in Christ Jesus has set us free from the law of sin and death."*[33] There is a key word in this verse that I want you to see; possibly the most important word in the entire verse. That word is "has;" it is past tense, which means that is already done. You are free from shame, free from guilt, and free from condemnation. If you are a child of God, don't let anyone or anything cause you to feel shame. If we sin, we don't hide, we repent. That does not mean that we go out and sin because we know we have repentance. It does mean, however, that we have repentance because God knew that we would sin. If God calls you out, if the Holy Spirit convicts you, it is because He wants you to repent. He doesn't convict you to mock you or to shame you; that is the work of the devil. Jesus is the one who redeems; Satan is the one who reminds. Don't be afraid of being called out; count it a blessing! Hebrews 12:6 tells us that the Lord chastens those whom He loves, and scourges every son whom He receives. I remember, as

---

[33] Romans 8:1, NKJV

Consensual Christianity

a young Christian, talking with my mother and describing to her the conviction I felt after doing something wrong. She gave me a very simple response that has stayed with me since that day. She said, "Son, you should only be worried if you stop feeling that way."

Afraid we may experience Him now but never again. During the journey to the Promised Land, the children of Israel questioned God several times saying, "why have you led us into the desert to die?". God had delivered them multiple times before. They saw His power in Egypt and experienced His glory on Mount Sinai, but they still had the thought that God was going to abandon them. They behaved as though they believed that the same God who was strong enough to deliver them out of captivity was not strong enough to sustain them in the wilderness. There are several things that we could identify as possible problems in the thinking of the Israelites, but the root of their issue is they viewed God through the lens of their circumstances instead of viewing their circumstances through God's eyes. I am guilty of doing the same thing and I am sure that I am not alone. We put God in a box when we act and think in this manner. We serve an infinite God but we try to understand Him with a finite mind. God is not confined by the impossible, in fact, that word does not exist to God. The only time that He even hears it is when we say it to Him. We act as though there is some mystical ritual or magic sequence of words we must say to make God "appear," but the truth is that He never leaves us or forsakes us. Being in His presence is our decision…it's our choice. Psalm 91 is one of my favorite chapters in the Bible. In it, the psalmist tells us how we get to make that choice, *"He who dwells in the secret place of the Most High shall abide under the shadow of the Almighty."*[34] The word, *dwell,* means to remain for a time, to live as a resident, to keep the attention directed. The word, *abide,* means to endure without yielding; to accept without objection. Think about that for a minute and let it sink in. The choice that we make is whether or not we are going to dwell in His secret place. If we live in God's presence we will be able to endure any trial without yielding. It is so easy to get distracted and discouraged by our circumstances though, isn't it? We need to put on some of those horse blinders so, no matter what is happening to the right or to the left, we can keep our attention directed towards the Father. That's what Jesus meant when He said, "seek ye first the kingdom of God and His righteousness, and all these things shall be added unto you."[35] Not only is it the key to living in God's presence, it is the fundamental principle to living a godly life. David went on to say in verse 2 of Psalm 91: "I will say of the Lord, He is my refuge and my fortress, my God, in Him will I trust." He knew, that if He stayed focused on God and trusted in Him, God would be his refuge and fortress. He didn't have to worry about a thing, God would provide. What is even better to me is what God says to David as an example to you and me: *"Because he has set his love upon me, therefore I will deliver him; I will set him on high because he has known My name. He shall call upon Me, and I will answer him. I will be with him*

---

34   Psalm 91:1, NKJV

35   Matthew 6:33, NKJV

in trouble; I will deliver him and honor him. With long life will I satisfy him and will show him My salvation."[36] God wants to speak that over us but we must first set our love upon Him. We must look to Him and in Him alone should we place our trust. Hebrews 11:6 says that God is a rewarder of those who diligently seek Him, so seek Him first and let Him worry about the rest.

The Second Most Powerful Word

How much power can there really be in a single word? By words, through faith, Jesus called Lazarus forth from the grave. I would say that was a pretty powerful act. So what exactly is the second most powerful word? It is a word that can completely stop all action, turn the most stable situation into one of uncertainty, and make confident men second-guess their very purpose and existence. The word is "but." I know, it is a small, insignificant word, but our words have power whether we realize it or not. Proverbs 18:21 says *"Death and Life are in the power of the tongue and those who love it will eat its fruit."* The tongue has the ability to speak. It is what we use to form the words that come out of our mouths. Whenever God speaks to us, He speaks life into us. When Jesus was being tempted by the devil, the devil said to Him "command this stone that it be made bread." Jesus responded, "man shall not live by bread alone but by every word of God." God's words bring life! The devil knows your circumstances and he will use those circumstances to distract you from God's promises. He knew that Jesus was hungry and he tried to use

---

36   Psalm 91:14-16, NKJV

that hunger to distract Jesus from the purpose and will of God. Jesus could have very easily turned the rock into bread but He knew that doing so would usurp God's sovereignty and authority in His life. When Jesus taught us to pray, He taught us to pray for God's provision and to acknowledge God's sovereignty. So in rejecting temptation Jesus was living by God's principles to attain God's promises.

We know that the most powerful word we could ever speak is the name of Jesus: the name above all names. The devil uses words also but when he speaks to you he only speaks from one perspective, his. His perspective brings loss, death, and destruction because he has come to steal, kill, and destroy, but Jesus came that we might have abundant life. Is "but" really the second most powerful word? As a conjunction, it is used to indicate possibility or uncertainty; as a preposition it means "with the exception of or barring all others;" as an adverb it means "to the contrary." So why is this one little word so powerful? This one little word has the power to stop the hand of God in your life but it also has the power to send demons fleeing.

Let's look at this word from two perspectives or in two situations. Situation one is in our conversations with God. Situation two is in our declarations to the devil. I know you are wondering what I mean by declarations to the devil so let me explain. When the devil talks to you (and he will talk to you), you need to talk back. Jesus did it, and if our master did it, what makes us think that we don't need to. Let's take a look at our conversation with God.

Consensual Christianity

Our Conversation with God: God speaks to His children on a continual basis and in the course of those conversations He reveals His will, purpose, and promises to us. When speaking with God we tend to use the word "but" as a conjunction; indicating alternate possibilities or our uncertainty in what He has said. With God, the word "but" moves us out of the realm of faith into the realm of fate. Faith says that my destiny is based on God's purpose, will, and promises; fate, on the other hand, says that my destiny is based on my circumstances. Faith is the power behind the words we speak, the call to action.

Hebrews 11:6 says that without faith it is impossible to please God, so here is what the devil does. God will speak to you through His word. As you begin to hold on to God's promises, they will cause faith and life to spring up on the inside of you. The devil then comes in and says, "but!" The devil's hope is that the word "but" will cause your focus to change from pressing on towards God's purpose to sitting idly by, worrying about your problems. If successful, he has turned your faith into doubt, your action into reaction, and your power into pity. You are now walking down the path of fate; saying that your circumstances control you as opposed to the journey of faith declaring the promises of God. The devil's goal is to completely dilute the word of God in your life. Why? It's simple, because God's word is a lamp unto your feet and a light unto your path; because faith comes by hearing the word of God; because with faith, you can please God. The devil knows that the more you grab ahold of God's word, the more you live by His principles and focus on

Chapter 4

His will, the more God can use you. So he tries to make you useless by filling you with doubt. Only doubt can hinder your faith and only a lack of faith can keep God from working in your life and in your situation. The good news is that we know how the devil will attack us, so now I am going to show you how to beat the devil at his game.

Our conversation with the devil: When the devil uses the word "but" with us he is trying to usurp God's power and authority in our lives. The devil does not have the ability to stop God from working on your behalf but you do. The devil will use you to do what he cannot do. So, we as believers have to beat him at his game and God has given us the weapons and the methods to do it. When the devil throws a "but" at you, throw one back!

In Ephesians 6, the apostle Paul talks about the armor of God: having your waist girded with truth, the breastplate of righteousness, the shield of faith, the helmet of salvation, and having your feet shod with the preparation of the gospel of peace. In all of the armor of God there is only one thing we use as a weapon: the Sword of the Spirit which is the Word of God. Everything else is for protection. The Word is a weapon; it is not for protection from the enemy, it is for attacking the enemy and defeating our flesh. Hebrews 4:12 says that the Word of God is quick and powerful and sharper than any two-edged sword, piercing even to the dividing asunder of soul and spirit, and of the joints and marrow, and is a discerner of the thought and intents of the heart. We have a weapon and we need to use it. Attack the devil; use the word of God against him. The shield

73

Consensual Christianity

of faith is great but don't spend your whole life blocking the fiery darts. Don't just sit back and let him attack you; fight back. God gave us His word to teach us how to defeat our flesh as well. We are saved but we are still human and will face all sorts of human temptations and fleshly lusts. God's word is our manual for living. It teaches us how to overcome the enemy and how to overcome our flesh.

Speak the word of God into every situation. It will build your faith (your shield) so you can block out the "buts" (fiery darts). Jesus was tempted just as we are. Jesus spoke the Word! Hebrews 4:15 says "for we do not have a high priest who cannot sympathize with our weaknesses, but was in all points tempted as we are, yet without sin." Speak the Word, speak the Word, speak the Word; make the devil pay for coming your way. As believers, we often lose sight of the power of our words. We are quick to give time and recognition to all that is wrong in our lives instead of focusing on all that God has and will continue to do in our lives. When we speak negatively, we are agreeing with the devil and contradicting God's word. Matthew 19:26 says that with God all things are possible. When the 12 disciples were saddened by the thought of Jesus leaving, Jesus told them that He would send the Helper. The Helper is the Holy Spirit. He lives inside of you and His power through you makes all things possible in your life. We need to start seeing ourselves through God's eyes but in order to accomplish this we must first start to speak over ourselves the things that God speaks over us. He said that we are His people, a royal priesthood and a holy nation. He did not say that we are broken, sick, and stupid. The Bible tells us that out of the abundance of the heart the mouth speaks so we need to fill our heart with God's word and His love. We should pray every day, "Lord, let me see myself the way you see me and let me see those around me the way you see them." We need to be filled with God's love and His word. If we fill ourselves with Him, when we open our mouths, He will flow out, and when He speaks He brings life. Speak God's word and speak life into your circumstances. Remember, if the devil throws a "but" at you, throw one back.

What have you promised God?

Have you ever found yourself making the statement, "Lord, if you just get me through this, I will..." Have you ever said that yourself or heard someone else say it? Why is it that we do this, promise God something in return for His help? I have even heard some of the most ungodly people promise God all types of things for His help in a time of crisis. So exactly what happens to these promises?

In Judges 11, we are told the story of a man named Jephthah. He was a mighty man of valor, a fighting man. At the time, Israel was constantly in battles; they had just defeated the Amorites and were turning their attention to the people of Ammon. The Bible says that Jephthah then made a vow with God. The dictionary defines the word "vow" as a solemn promise or assertion; specifically, one by which a person is

Consensual Christianity

bound to an act, service, or condition. So we offer God a quid pro quo. We say, "God, if you do this for me, I will do that for you." So Jephthah made God an offer; he said "If you will indeed deliver the people of Ammon into my hands, then it will be that whatever comes out of the doors of my house to meet me, when I return in peace from the people of Ammon, shall surely be the Lords and I will offer it as a burnt offering." The Bible says that the people of Ammon were subdued before the children of Israel, 20 cities, all delivered into his hands just as he asked.

So God was faithful to His part of the vow. I'm willing to bet that Jephthah rejoiced from the end of the battle all the way back home. He was serving the one, true God; the One who could defeat any enemy. He rejoiced all the way home until he saw what or should I say who came out of the door. I am convinced that at the time he made the vow he truly did not believe or even consider that it would be his daughter; his only child, that would come to meet him. Can you imagine? I know that his joy immediately turned into sorrow. Judges 11:39 says, "He carried out his vow with her whom he had vowed."

Before we go on, let me say that I do not believe God allowed Jephthah to sacrifice his daughter. God has never accepted a human sacrifice. I have read several scholarly explanations of what occurred and most agree that Jephthah probably gave his daughter in service to the temple. This may not seem like a big sacrifice to you or me but let's consider two things. First, those given in service to the temple were never

76

allowed to marry, meaning there was no chance she would ever have children. Secondly, consider that this was Jephthah's only child, his only chance for his lineage to continue.

Truthfully, I don't believe that Jephthah even needed to make the vow. God had already promised the land to Abraham, Isaac, and Jacob; even to Moses. All the children of Israel had to do was live according to God's law. The land was already theirs but he felt he had to make a vow to possess it. Why, you may ask. It's simple, because of disobedience.

Judges 16:28 says, "Samson called to the Lord saying, O Lord God, remember me I pray; strengthen me, I pray, just this once, O God, that I may with one blow take vengeance on the Philistines for my two eyes!" Then Samson took hold of the pillars that supported the temple and knocked them down. The temple collapsed, and Samson, along with the Philistines, perished. Samson lost his anointing because of disobedience. Chapter fifteen of Judges talks about Samson killing thousands of Philistines; one man can only over take thousands with the anointing. Without the anointing, Samson was just a man; and as a man he made a vow, a plea for the anointing to return so he could repay those who had done him wrong. Truth of the matter is that disobedience not only cost Samson the anointing on his life, it also costs him his two eyes and eventually his life.

Here we have two examples of how disobedience costs these men what they valued most. Jephthah lost his daughter because of the disobedience of Israel and Samson lost his life because of his own disobedience. Now I know that the Bible

Consensual Christianity

does not specifically say that these things happened because of disobedience but the reason I draw that conclusion is this: In Genesis 12, God promised Abram (Abraham) land and many descendants, a great nation. Jephthah made a vow trying to possess what God had already promised to Abraham. The reason the promise had not yet been fulfilled is because of the disobedience of the descendants of Abraham. Our disobedience is what keeps us from possessing God's promises. We make "vows" as an attempt to get back into God's good graces in the hopes that He will respond and help us obtain what He has promised.

God is not interested in our vows or pleas to do what is right in return for His rescue. That is not what He wants. God is interested in two things: our faith and our obedience. Genesis 26:4-5 says *"And I will make your descendants multiply as the stars of heaven; I will give to your descendants all these lands; and in your seed all the nations of the earth shall be blessed; because Abraham obeyed my voice and kept My charge, My statutes, My commandments, and My laws."* Notice that it does not say that because Abraham made a vow or promised God something but to the contrary it was because of Abraham's obedience that he was blessed. Hebrews 11 talks about the great men of faith and all that they accomplished through faith. Not once does it mention any kind of quid pro quo between them and God. Why, because they understood the importance of listening to God's voice and believing His word. They trusted God even though they could not see the promises. Hebrews 11:1 says that faith is the substance of things hoped

78

for, the evidence of things not seen.

I would say that, for us, faith is obedience to God's principles on our journey to fulfilling His will for our lives; seeking God's kingdom first and trusting that He will take care of the things we need. Faith is obedience to God's word even when we can't comprehend it. The just shall live by faith. Without faith it is impossible to please God. Jesus is the author and finisher of our faith; and by faith we are saved through grace. Faith and obedience are what makes us who we are as children of God. Think about it: Hebrews 11:6 *"but without faith it is impossible to please God for he who comes to God must believe that He is, and that He is a rewarder of those that diligently seek Him."* Without Faith it is impossible to please God. God is not interested in our vows and our promises; He wants our faith and our obedience. He wants us to trust in His word enough to follow it without question. Obey His commandments, have faith in His promises, and follow His principles. You will never find yourself needing a quid pro quo with the Almighty because obedience is better than sacrifice.

You Get Out What You Put In:

This chapter covered a lot of information and although that information was given in several different ways, it was really about two main points: the importance of maintaining your temple and the cost of disobedience. If you think about it, the two really do go hand in hand. Proper maintenance of our temple is an act of obedience. On the topic of temple maintenance, whenever engaged in a conversation about movies,

Consensual Christianity

books, TV, and music, and what is considered appropriate for Christians to watch or listen to, I give two responses. The first one is an eating analogy based on my personal experience. The second one is Philippians 4:8.

First, let's talk about the food analogy. In high school I was an athlete. I played soccer and basketball, and I ran track; all at a fairly competitive level. Each coach I played for gave us pretty specific instructions about what we should and should not eat since the things we consumed would have an effect on our performance, either positively or negatively. No athlete can be successful for long if all they eat is hot dogs and cookies. Hot dogs and cookies are acceptable occasionally, but to stay in peak shape and to perform at a high level the athlete needs to eat a healthy, well balanced diet. Now, pretend the things you watch, read, and listen to are spiritual food. If you want to stay in peak shape, you need to consume healthy foods. Too much junk will diminish your performance and eventually render you ineffective. Does that mean that you should never listen to secular music? No, but it should not be all that you listen to. The majority of what you listen to should be music that glorifies God and edifies your spirit. With that being said, if you are struggling in some area of your spiritual life, you may want to go on a strict diet. There have been times in my life where I have dedicated myself to prayer for a specific reason so I cut out anything that did not glorify God. Just like a person who is on a diet for medical reasons, there are times where a spiritual diet may be a matter of spiritual life and death. Satan will use whatever means at his

80

disposal to defeat you. Sometimes the best defense is to remove as many of his means as possible.

This is where Philippians 4:8 comes in. The Apostle Paul tells us, "Brethren, whatever things are true, whatever things are noble, whatever things are just, whatever things are pure, whatever things are lovely, whatever things are of good report, if there is any virtue and if there is anything praiseworthy - meditate on these things." The truth of the matter is that spiritual junk food will stunt your spiritual growth. If you have ever gone on a diet or any weight-loss program, you know that junk food always hinders your progress and keeps you from your goals. In Philippians 4:8, Paul was showing us what a healthy spiritual diet looks like.

I'm not going to talk about the cost of disobedience here because we talk about the importance of obedience and the effects of sin in the following chapter, so just stay tuned. I hope you can see how important it is to consume that which is healthy for you spiritually. Also, I hope I did not lose you in the midst of my analogy. If so, I apologize. Just know that what you get out what you put in. If you are constantly feeding yourself visions of illicit sex, drugs, cursing, and other images of sin, that is where your thoughts will dwell. Don't make the devil's job any easier!

Consensual Christianity

5

Happily Ever After

Blessed is the man who walks not in the counsel of the ungodly, nor stands in the path of sinners, nor sits in the seat of the scornful; but his delight is in the law of the Lord, and in His law he meditates day and night.

Psalm 1:1-2

Consensual Christianity

Like many married couples, my wife and I have experienced good times and bad times. It does not take long for married couples to figure out what things they do and do not like about their spouse. While dating, everyone puts their best foot forward. Early in marriage, everyone goes through a honeymoon period where the newness of the marriage and the love for your spouse allows you to overlook things that would otherwise bother you. But, after some time has passed, you begin to notice that they leave their clothes on the floor or put the toilet paper on the roller in the opposite direction than you do. These little things that you overlooked for months, maybe even years suddenly become an issue.

My wife and I had been married for 12 years at the time I completed this book. Overall, we have enjoyed a wonderful marriage, one that many of our friends try to emulate. I love to talk with couples who have been married for a long time. I like to ask them what they think has caused their marriage to be successful. I typically get three answers: love, patience, and communication. Love, not the mushy fall in and out of love type of love, but the committed and devoted type of love that is willing to face any obstacle. The kind of love that causes you to put the hopes, dreams, wants and needs of your spouse above your own. Next, they have patience enough to understand that everyone has a bad day every now and then. The kind of patience that teaches you to endure the bad days and embrace them as opportunities to show your spouse just how committed you are to them. Lastly, they have the type of communication that does not cease but knows when to talk and when to listen. As we talked about in chapter 2, communication is a large part of the quality time that fuels every relationship.

I remember one evening in particular that my wife and I had a little disagreement. I walked into our bedroom where she was watching TV. I asked her a question and she snapped at me. I did what every good husband does, I snapped back. That was not a good idea! I felt justified in my response because she actually had a little bit of an attitude for several days. After our little encounter, I went into the closet to pray. That may sound funny to you but I often prayed in our closet because it was dark and secluded. It was an easy place for me to block out everything else and focus on God. After all, it is hard to get distracted by old shoes and dresses. Well, I had a difficult time praying that night. I could not think of anything to say. Then the Holy Spirit spoke to me. He told me to go apologize to my wife. Initially, I resisted because I felt justified in my position. Her attitude was unwarranted. After a few minutes, I realized that He was not going to let this go, I complied, albeit somewhat reluctantly.

I walked out of the closet and said, "Honey, I need to talk to you. I owe you an apology for responding to you the way I did. You are my wife and I should always respond to you in a loving and respectful manner." Immediately she began to cry and said, "No, it is actually me who owes you the apology. I realize I have been in a bad mood for a few days now. I have been having a really rough time at work and I don't know what to do about it. I guess I allowed my frustration there to spill out on to you." I accepted her apology, kissed her on the forehead and reassured her that she could always vent to me when needed. The Holy Spirit taught me two lessons that day. First, our disagreement occurred because of a failure to communicate. I noticed the change in my wife's demeanor but never asked what was going on. She was having a rough time with something but didn't talk to me about it. If we had taken the time to communicate before the disagreement, the disagreement would not have happened. Second, this one is for all the men out there, husbands should always respond to their wives in a caring and loving manner, regardless of the circumstances. I have learned that God likes to use men, His men, as the catalyst for change in the home. Truthfully, husbands and wives should always talk to one another in a caring and loving manner but men especially need to be aware of this. *1 Peter 3:7 says, "Husbands, likewise dwell with them (your wives) with understanding, giving honor to the wife, as to the weaker vessel, and as being heirs together of the grace of life, that your prayers may not be hindered."* Communication is an essential part of a successful marriage.

You may be wondering what that story has to do with developing a relationship with God. Well, the Bible uses marriage as an example of our relationship with God. Marriage is a covenant act between the husband, wife, and God. There are many parallels between marriage and our relationship with God. The church is the body and bride of Christ. Also, what image comes to mind when you think about the title of this chapter, *Happily Ever After?* Our relationship with God, just like a marriage, requires love, patience, and communication to be successful.

This chapter is all about discovering the purpose in your relationship with God. You were created on purpose and for a purpose. Whether you realize it or not, you are a new creation. You are not the same old person you used to be. The Holy Spirit of God dwells inside of you. It would be impossible for you to remain the same with such a powerful presence in your life. You have been changed and are being changed. For some, the process (known as sanctification) is easier than others. If you are like me, you don't always pick up on the lessons God is teaching you the first time around. I have had to repeat quite a few lessons in life. But this journey, your journey, is a journey of purpose.

One of the most encouraging things to me as a Christian is to know that I am not alone. Even the Apostles made mistakes and had to be sanctified as they went through life. Peter denied Christ and had to be restored. Paul said that his flesh and spirit constantly struggled and he found himself doing the things he did not want to do. You are not alone. Romans 3:23 reminds us that all have sinned and fall short of God's glory. We are not perfect. We are, however, in relationship with a perfect God, filled with His perfect Spirit, and redeemed by the blood of His perfect Son. All we have to do is move forward as we abide in Him. In this chapter, we will discuss moving forward with God by learning to listen to and know God's voice, to believe what

Consensual Christianity

God says about us, the importance of our obedience, and the effects of sin in our life and in our relationship with Him. Let's start by learning to listen to and know God's voice.

Listening to and knowing God's voice

Have you ever been in a store and heard a child cry? If you are a parent, your initial thoughts are, "where is my child and are they ok?" Immediately, every parent in earshot stops what they are doing and listens, trying to determine the distance and direction from which the cry came. As soon as they realize that their child is not the one that is crying, most return to what they were doing. Some will continue to investigate to determine what is going on, but most just keep it moving. If you happen to be the parent of the crying child, your response is different than the other parents. Everything in you starts to analyze the situation as you go into response mode. I have wondered how it is, that in the midst of a crowded place, a parent can distinguish the sound of their child from all the others. My wife and I have five children so we have to distinguish five different sounds. That can be a little overwhelming at times, but we are able to be successful because of the time that we spend with our children. We know the sound of each individual cry and each individual voice because we have taken the time to learn them. I can even tell you, based on their tone, just how serious the situation may be.

The opposite is also true. My children know how to

respond based on the tone of my voice. They know when things are serious and they need to respond immediately. They also know when I am playing and they can have a little fun. Our relationship with our heavenly Father should be no different. In fact, it can be the same way, but it requires the same catalyst. Time! So, why do we have trouble figuring out "who" is speaking to us? How can we determine when it is God and how to respond?

In John 10, we read about Jesus, the Good Shepherd. Jesus said, *"My sheep hear my voice, and I know them, and they follow me"*[37] Prior to that, he said, *"They will by no means follow a stranger, but will flee from him, for they do not know the voice of strangers."*[38] How do we know when God is speaking to us? This is something I have definitely struggled with in the past. I would ask myself, "was that God or did I just think that up?" I would think to myself, "Perhaps the devil is trying to deceive me or lead me astray." How can we know for sure if we are hearing God's voice or just making up stuff as we go along? Truthfully, I still have moments when I struggle with this, though not nearly as much as I used to. Rest assured, we can know God's voice and we can be certain we are hearing Him and not our own thoughts, or the words of the devil.

The first step is to abide in Him. John 15:4 says *"abide in Me, and I in you. As the branch cannot bear fruit of itself, unless it abides in the vine; neither can you, unless you abide in Me."* When you hear

---

37   John 10:27, NKJV

38   John 10:5, NKJV

Consensual Christianity

God's voice but you feel unsure, ask yourself whether or not the voice you heard told you something that produces fruit? If not, it is not of God. If it does, chances are that it is God speaking to you. Producing fruit does not always mean it is what you want to hear. It could in fact be the last thing you expected to hear. The question of producing fruit is focused on the end result, not the immediate response. In verse two of John 15, Jesus says that every branch, that does not bear fruit, God removes. When God speaks to you, the thing that He asks you to do will produce good fruit, and that fruit will bring Him glory. God is interested in our growth. He wants us to be productive for His kingdom. Everything that He asks of you will fall in line with His word. Numbers 23:19 says, *"God is not a man that He should lie or the son of man that He should change His mind."* He will never contradict His word.

The second step is to ask yourself, "does this cause my faith to grow or create doubt?" Now, let me caution you for a second. You may hear something from God that makes you say, "Seriously God, you want me to do what? How am I supposed to do that?" These are common questions you may have when God asks you to do something, especially if it is something big. Mary, the mother of Jesus, asked a similar question when the angel told her that she was going to give birth to Jesus. Her exact response was, "How can this be, since I do not know a man?" The angel went on to tell her that God was going to make it happen (I'm paraphrasing). Upon hearing this Mary responded, "Behold the maidservant of the Lord! Let it be to me according to your word."[39] Do you see how Mary's initial response was to question how she would be able to do what God was asking of her? This is a perfectly normal response so do not be discouraged if your immediate response is the same. Do you also see how, upon hearing that God was in control and that He was going to make this possible, Mary's uncertainty went away? She simply said let it be done as the Lord has said. This caused her faith to grow.

The flip side of this is doubt. James 1:6-8 says, *"but let him who asks ask in faith, with no doubting, for he who doubts is like a wave of the sea driven and tossed by the wind. For let not that man suppose that he will receive anything from the Lord; he is a double-minded man, unstable in all his ways."* The devil is the author of doubt. He uses doubt to stop our action. If the voice you hear is generating doubt, rebuke it. A word from God brings life, it causes our faith to spring up. I know that sometimes we worry about the way something may come to pass. There is a difference between wondering how God will make something happen and doubting that He can make it happen. It is perfectly normal to wonder if you are capable of doing what God has asked. The truth of the matter is that we are not capable of fulfilling His word on our own, but only by the power of His Holy Spirit will it come to pass. We should never doubt God. He did not make a mistake when He chose you to be His vessel. With God, all things are possible.

The third step is to ask yourself, "does this thing glorify God or something else, maybe even me?" Going back to John

---

39   Luke 1:34-38

15, if you look at verses 7and 8, Jesus said *"If you abide in Me and My words abide in you, you will ask what you desire and it shall be done for you. By this My Father is glorified, that you bear much fruit; so you will be My disciples."* Our purpose in being here is to bring glory and honor to God. If what you are hearing or doing does not bring glory and honor to Him then it is not of Him. When we glorify Him, He in turn glorifies us. God will never ask you to do something that shames you or brings dishonor to Him.

If you abide in Him, He will tell you His will for your life; your purpose in being. In the will of God there is peace, joy, hope, and rest. Matthew 11:28-30 says *"Come to me, all you who labor and are heavy laden and I will give you rest. Take My yoke upon you and learn from Me for I am gentle and lowly in heart and you will find rest for your souls. For My yoke is easy and My burden is light."* I believe that Jesus is telling us to follow His will for our lives so we can have peace. Peace does not tell me that I will not have trouble; to the contrary, it means that I will have joy in the midst of the trouble by His grace. The first step in knowing God's voice is abiding in Him. Abide, according to the dictionary, means to endure without yielding or to accept without objection. In other words, seek Him without yielding, never hesitate to go after Him, pursue Him with all of your heart, soul, and strength. Second, when God speaks to you it will build your faith. Romans 10:17 says *"Faith comes by hearing and hearing by the WORD of God."* Jesus is the living word that speaks life, His life, into you causing your faith to multiply. You will know that the word is from God because He will give you the strength to believe, the grace to obey, and the faith to act. People around you may think that this journey you are embarking on is impossible, but with God all things are possible. Satan can only distort the possible, but my God is Lord over the impossible; He can control any circumstance and bend it to His will.

Lastly, if God speaks a word to you, it will ultimately glorify Him. In the last days of His earthly life, Jesus was speaking with two of His disciples and said "Now my soul is troubled and what shall I say? Father, save me from this hour; but for this purpose I came to this hour. Father, glorify your name." Jesus knew that His purpose was to glorify the Father. If we are truly His disciples, that is our purpose as well. As our master, He will only instruct us to do the same as Him. Amen!

Living by the Word

So, what exactly does God say about His children? What has He said about you and me? For starters, He says:
- We are called into the fellowship of His Son (1 Corinthians 1:19)
- We are His heirs and joint heirs with Christ (Romans 8:17)
- We are His sons (Romans 8:19)
- We are His chosen people (1 Peter 2:9)

We are His heirs, His children, His chosen people, a royal priesthood and a holy nation. We are His chosen people. WOW!!! We are His. I don't know about you but the fact that God chose me blows my mind. It's one thing to think that I searched and found Him but to think that, in the midst of all my mess, He chose me; unfathomable. Before time began he predestined me, He predestined you. I am a joint heir with Christ. I am a child of God. I could keep on saying that all day. Although I know what God has said about me and how He feels about me, I don't always act like it. Sometimes I question it. I'm a little ashamed to admit that. Why is that? Why is it that I can say I am a child of God but act like a child of doubt and pity? I know that 1 Peter 2:24 says that by the stripes Jesus bore, I was healed. It does not say that I might be healed but that I was healed. The word "was" means that it is already done. So why do I walk around acting broken and feeling damaged? I know that Matthew 11:28 says that if I come to Him and take His burden, He will give me rest; so why do I walk around mentally, spiritually, and emotionally tired. See, it is one thing to know the Word of God but it is something completely different to believe it and live it.

Knowing the Word of God is important; it builds our faith. Faith is the life-blood of any believer. Romans 10:17 says that faith comes by hearing the Word of God. Faith comes by knowing the good news of the gospel of Christ. The Word is a lamp unto our feet and a light unto our path. It guides us, it teaches us how to live, and it teaches us how to withstand the attacks of the enemy. Knowing the Word of God is great but even an atheist can know the word of God. Satan himself can tell you what is in the Bible. So as believers, it goes beyond simply knowing the Word of God, we have to live it, but before we can live it we have to believe it.

94

Isaiah 53:1 says, *"Who has believed our report and to whom has the arm of the Lord been revealed?"* Belief is the bridge that covers the gap between knowing the Word of God and living the Word of God. Believing is one half of the salvation equation. The Bible says that in order to be saved you must believe with your heart and confess with your mouth. It does not say to think you know in your heart, or to think about it in your mind; it says you must believe it. Hebrews 11:6 says, *"Without faith it is impossible to please God, for he who comes to God must believe that He is, and that He is a rewarder of those who diligently seek Him."* It is impossible for us to please God if we do not believe.

The difference between being someone who knows about Jesus and someone who believes in Jesus is the difference between heaven and hell, life and death, healing and brokenness, joy and depression, peace and despair. The difference between knowing and believing is that true belief implies trust. God wants us to trust Him. Trust Him enough to know that His Word is sure and His promises are true. Trust Him more than you trust in your own intellect. Believe in His promises instead of believing in the progression of your circumstances. We serve a God that cannot lie. If He said He will deliver you then guess what, HE WILL DELIVER YOU!

Belief in itself is not enough for me as it pertains to God's word. I want to live His word. I want to be a living example of His word. James 1:22 says, *"Be ye doers of the Word and not hearers only, deceiving yourselves."* Knowing is one thing, believing is great, but living the Word is the purpose and calling

95

of everyone who claims to believe. Knowing God's word builds our faith and causes us to believe, but being faithful requires action. James 2:26 says that just as the body without the spirit is dead, so faith without works is also dead.

So, how do we live God's word? The answer lies in the difference between knowing what God says about you and believing what God says about you. The difference is trust. Trust allows us to step out in faith and live, not to achieve the promises, but according to the promises of God because they are already ours. We don't have to achieve them, all we have to do is possess them. We live God's word by focusing on His promises instead of submitting to our problems. Does this mean that we ignore our problems or pretend they don't exist? No, but it does mean that we place our faith in God and move forward without fear, knowing that He will always be faithful to never leave us or forsake us. We live out God's word by acting like children of God instead of slaves of circumstance. We live out God's word by knowing, believing, and acting according to His word, not in spite of His word. We walk by faith and not by sight; we become doers and not just hearers; we live like heirs to an unshakable kingdom, the kingdom of God. We are a chosen people, a royal priesthood, a holy nation, God's children, and His very own. We live like we belong to God and not to the world. We live God's word by faith. Our faith shows God that we trust Him. The just, according to Hebrews 10:38, shall live by faith. Without faith, it is impossible to live according to His word, and if we do not live according to His word, we cannot follow His commandments.

Don't just know the Word, believe the Word, and once you believe it, live it! We serve a life giving God. Jesus is the Word made manifest, the Living Word. The Word of God is alive and fresh and new every morning. These are not just words on a page to be memorized. They are life, abundant and rejuvenating. The Word teaches us how to live and how to fight the enemy. The Word is our weapon, sharper than any two edged sword. Live the Word. Incorporate it into every fiber of your being, every second of every minute of every hour of every day of your life. The Word gives us God's promises for His people, the ones He has already fulfilled and the ones we need to possess. Live the Word and let it live inside of you.

The Importance of Obedience

When God speaks to us, He listens closely and watches carefully. He is interested in how we respond to His voice and to His word. As a Father, when I ask my kids to do something, the way they respond determines my responses to them and how they are rewarded. If I get a simple "yes, sir" and they begin their task their reward will be good. If they do what they are asked with a poor attitude or if they do not do what they are asked, not only will they not receive a reward, but there will also be some severe consequences. God handles us the same way; a good example of this is the principle of giving.

2 Corinthians 7:6-7 says "*He which sows sparingly shall reap also sparingly; and he which sows bountifully shall reap also bountifully.*

Consensual Christianity

Every man accordingly, as he purposes in his heart, so let him give; not grudgingly or of necessity: for God loves a cheerful giver." This passage gives us a valuable glimpse into the heart of God and teaches us about more than just giving. When I read this these verses I realize that God is not only concerned with my obedience; He is deeply concerned with the attitude of my obedience. Why, you may ask? The answer is simple: the attitude of our obedience shows the true intent and condition of our heart. Reluctant obedience is not what God is looking for; He is after our willing submission to His will. In fact, I would venture to say that reluctant obedience or delayed obedience is tantamount to disobedience.

There are two principles that run parallel throughout the Bible, faith and obedience. Hebrews 11:6 says that without faith it is impossible to please God. So if our faith pleases Him, what does our obedience do? Obedience displays our love for God, our willingness to submit to His authority, and our spiritual maturity. It shows God that we can handle more responsibilities. Throughout the Bible God gives us principles for life. The result of following those principles is receiving the benefits of obedience. Some promises are attained immediately and some are eternal but the result is the same; we receive His rewards. We do not obey to simply receive rewards, our motivation to obey should be to please our heavenly Father...the rewards should be the icing on the cake. In fact, we should be so motivated to obey that we willingly submit to Him whether we believe we will receive anything or not. We love Him because He first loved us

(1 John 4:19).

In 1 Kings 13, we are told the story of the man of God. 1 Kings 13:8 says, *"And the man of God said unto the king, if thou would give me half of your house, I would not go with you, neither will I eat bread or drink water in this place. For so it was charged me by the Word of the Lord saying 'Eat no bread, nor drink water, nor turn again by the same way you came.'* So the man of God received a command from the Lord to deliver a message to the king and he was instructed to not eat, drink water, or return from the way he came. He was obedient, at least at first. Then in verse 18 an old prophet came to him and said, *"an angel of the Lord came to me and spoke to me by the word of the Lord saying 'Bring him back so he can eat bread and drink water."* So he did.

Before we go on, I want to draw your attention to something. God gave the man of God direct instructions. If God spoke to him directly about the king, why did he not expect God to speak to him directly about himself. If you have a relationship with God, He will speak to you directly. Does that mean that God does not speak to us through other people? No, but in my personal experience that only occurs for two reasons. First, it is to confirm something that God has already told me directly and ease any sense of uncertainty I may be having about what I was told. Secondly, God has been trying to speak to me but I have been too distracted or purposely not listening. In both cases, the words spoken to me were a confirmation of something I already knew in my spirit, not brand new information.

Consensual Christianity

Now, back to the man of God; if you continue reading through verse 26, God speaks to the man of God through the old prophet about his disobedience and he ends up being killed by a lion on his way home. Disobeying God's word not only opens the door to consequences but it also moves you out of the will of God. Being out of God's will places you outside of His provision and, in some cases, His protection. Now, being eaten by a lion is a pretty severe consequence and most likely not one that you or I will have to face. However, think about this, Peter says the devil roams about as a roaring lion seeking whom he may devour. Disobedience leaves you more susceptible to the attack of the enemy and weakens your ability to stand firm in the midst of the attack. All throughout the Bible are examples of the fact that disobedience leads to negative consequences.

As a result of disobedience, Moses was not allowed to enter the Promised Land. David was rebuked by the prophet, Nathan, when God spoke through him saying, *"Now, therefore the sword will never depart from your house because you despised me and took the wife of Uriah the Hittite to be your own. This is what the Lord says: Out of your own household I am going to bring calamity upon you. Before your very eyes I am going to take your wives and give them to one who is close to you and he will lie with your wives in broad daylight. You did it in secret but I will do this in broad daylight, before all of Israel."*[40] Disobedience breeds consequences. Sin is any act of disobedience. The consequence of sin is death, separation from God. To be close to God, we must obey. God wants our obedience.

---

[40]   2 Samuel 12:10-12, NKJV

Chapter 5

Just as disobedience has consequences, obedience has rewards. *"Looking unto Jesus, the author and finisher of our faith, who for the joy that was set before Him endured the cross, despising the shame, and is seated at the right hand of the throne of God."*[41] Jesus was obedient, even through the pain and shame of the cross, because He knew His reward. "For the joy that was set before Him;" He knew the results of His obedience and so do we. God promises us long life if we honor our parents. He promises us abundance if we sow abundantly. He promises us eternal life if we accept His gift of salvation. He promises us peace if we trust in Him. He promises to never leave us nor forsake us. All we have to do is be obedient to His Word. The reason we cannot please God without faith is because we cannot truly be obedient to His principles without having faith in His promises. God tells us the rewards as motivation for the hard times. Rewards are not the reason to be obedient they are the motivation to obey. We should obey because we serve a God who has our best interest at heart. Jeremiah 29:11 says, *'For I know the thoughts I have for you,' declares the Lord; 'Plans to prosper you and not to harm you, to give you a hope and a future."* While this passage of Scripture was spoken directly to the nation of Israel, I believe the underlying principle applies to us. God does not want to harm us; He wants us to live abundant lives, full of His grace and His mercy. God asks for our obedience because He knows that His plan will give us far more than our plans ever could. The consequences of disobedience are there to show us that God has a better way, a better plan,

41 Hebrews 12:2, NKJV

than anything humanly fathomable. All we have to do is live a life of obedience to His word, and obedience to His will.

The Effects of Sin

"For the wages of sin is death but the gift of God is eternal life in Christ Jesus our Lord." Romans 6:23

As a child, I was physically and sexually abused. Consequently, as an older teen / young adult, I had a lot of scars and brokenness to deal with. The physical abuse left me fearful of a lot of things. I hid it well, only a few around me knew the turmoil I felt on the inside. I missed out on a lot of good opportunities because I allowed fear to dictate my decisions. The sexual abuse left me confused. As a misguided young man, I assumed, and feared, that being sexually assaulted by a male somehow made me gay. I decided that I had to sleep around with as many women as possible, in order to prove I wasn't gay. I know how preposterous that sounds, but sin is never logical.

Like I said, I was confused...very confused. I was also very hurt and very broken. My dysfunctional childhood had damaged me in ways that I did not understand. As you can see, my thinking was very flawed. I was justifiably hurt and broken. My anger was even justified, but my sin was not. I used the sins committed against me as justification for the sins I was committing. The people who wronged me will have to give an account for their actions. Likewise, I had to give an account for mine.

For years, I committed sin after sin after horrible sin, all in the name of my own brokenness. I felt justified, like I deserved to be able to do the things I was doing. I hurt a lot of people in the process, people that did not deserve to be hurt. Fear and pain ruled my life. Eventually, I found myself addicted to sex and pornography; trapped and struggling to hold on to life itself. It was during this period that I avoided going to church and anything that had to do with God. I was screwed up and saw no way out. I was so broken that I eventually tried to take my own life. It was at this point that I began to realize what was wrong with me, sin. I was in bondage to sin; sin that was killing me spiritually and physically.

I was angry and hurt. Bitterness had taken root in my heart, bitterness towards all of the people that had hurt me. Sex was my outlet, a way of self-medicating. Some turn to drugs and alcohol, some turn to gambling and other reckless behaviors as a means of alleviating pain, but all of these things just lead to more pain and hurt. I stopped worshipping God and started worshipping my hurt. Fear, pain, and hurt were all idols in my life; idols that had taken the place of God in my life. They had to be torn down in order for God to reclaim His rightful place in my heart.

I'm going to stop there for a moment and change direction a little bit. I have spoken with plenty of people who have been abused in some way. I know what it feels like to feel abandoned and used. I also know what it feels like to feel unloved and unlovable. God loves you! God wants you to know His love, He wants to mend your brokenness, and He wants to give you peace. God is love and perfect love casts out all fear, you don't have to be afraid. Trust in God! Trust in God! Trust in God! Give you hurts to Him and let Him do what only He can. There is nothing that can fill the voids in your life the way that God can.

When we allow sin to take root in our lives, it has an impact. Sin separates us from God, the only one who can heal us. As we begin to pursue sin, we lose focus on the one we should be pursuing, God. Sin always leads to more sin which leads to eventual spiritual death as Romans 6:23 states.

So, what are the effects of sin? To understand its effects, we must first understand what sin actually is. The dictionary defines sin as: *a transgression of the law of God; a vitiated state of human nature in which the self is estranged from God.*[42] The word vitiated means "to make ineffective." Sin is also referred to as transgression. Transgression is defined as the act or process of violating a command or law. We can surmise, based on the aforementioned definitions that sin is the act or process of violating God's law that renders us ineffective and separates us from God. Sin is an act that weakens our spiritual man and separates us from the only one who has the power to restore us, God.

Sin is very simple in its nature, but very complex in its process. That statement may sound a little convoluted, but I intend to explain. Sin, in its nature is an act that violates God's law and separates us from God; simple, right? No, it's not quite that simple. Sin starts long before we get to the actual act. Sin, if we think about it and are willing to admit, is usually the result of us placing the desires of our flesh above God. We lie because our flesh wants to avoid conflict, consequences, or embarrassment. We steal because our flesh wants something that does not belong to it and we don't have the means to acquire.

Sin usually starts as a temptation. A temptation is the desire to do something contrary to God's law. Temptation, however, in and of itself is not sin. I repeat, it is not a sin to be tempted. If so, Jesus would not have been a perfect sacrifice to satisfy God's wrath toward our sin. In addition, God does not tempt us. James 1:13 says, *Let no one say when he is tempted, I am being tempted by God," for God cannot be tempted by evil nor does He himself tempt anyone."* God is not the author of temptation. Is Satan responsible for tempting us? Yes, but only to a certain degree. The Bible refers to him as the deceiver and the accuser of the brethren. Satan usually deceives us into thinking our sins are justified and accuses us when we do sin. This is not to say that Satan does not tempt us, quite the contrary. He plays on our temptation through deception, using trickery to cause us to fall further into temptation.

Satan is not omniscient (all-knowing), omnipotent (all-powerful), or omnipresent (all places at all times). Only God can claim those attributes. As such, he (Satan) is not able to tempt all of us at the same time. His demons do not possess those

Consensual Christianity

attributes either, so tempting everyone would be a daunting task for them. If we took an honest look at our lives we would all have to admit that we usually do their job for them, or at least make their job easy. On a side note, I'm not even sure if Satan has to worry about tempting the unsaved. This is just my opinion so do not take this as theologically sound doctrine. The Bible teaches that, prior to salvation, we are slaves in bondage to sin. In my opinion, it is only those who are free that Satan has to concern himself with, not those who are still in his camp.

Satan uses one main ploy in his attempts to deceive us. As we discussed in the section, "The Second Most Powerful Word," Satan will usually distort God's word to trick you or to cause you to doubt. He did the same thing to Jesus. Matthew 4:6, *"and he said to Him, 'If you are the Son of God, throw Yourself down. For it is written: He shall give His angels charge over you', and 'In their hands they shall bear you up, lest you dash your foot against a stone.'"* Satan tried the same thing in the Garden of Eden, albeit successful that time, when he deceived Eve.

So, if temptation does not come from God, and the devil is only partially responsible, then who or what tempts us? Much to our own chagrin, we tempt ourselves. The same passage of Scripture we looked at previously in James 1:13 goes on to say in James 1:14-15, *"But each one is tempted when he is drawn away by his own desires and enticed. Then, when desire has conceived, it gives birth to sin, and sin when it is full-grown, brings forth death."* There is a process to sin. It doesn't just happen as we would sometimes like to think. Understanding the process is a great tool in overcoming sin in

106

our lives. If we know that temptation is the start of the process, then we know when to nip it in the bud so to speak. The further along we allow it to get in the process, the harder it is to stop. The act is the conception of desire the gives birth to sin.

Let me give you a real life example that hits a little close to home for many married couples. Adultery never just happens. It usually starts because something is not right at home and the couple does not address it. One member of the marriage then meets an individual who happens to fill the void that is left by the dysfunction in the marriage. The temptations are the "what if" thoughts or the "I wish thoughts." You know, "What if my husband was more like him?" or "I wish my wife treated me the way that she does." This is a great time to exercise 1 Corinthians 10:12-13:

Therefore let him who thinks he stands take heed lest he fall. Not temptation has overtaken you except such as is common to man; but God is faithful, who will not allow you to be tempted beyond what you are able, but with the temptation will also make the way of escape, that you may be able to bear it.

God makes a way of escape…we need to take it.

In 2006, my wife and I hit a small rough patch in our marriage. Out of respect for her, I will not give any details on what the rough patch was other than to say that it was difficult for us. The situation I described in the previous paragraph began to play out in my life. There was a particular lady who started paying a little extra attention to me at work. Within a couple of weeks, I found myself having the thought, "I really wish my wife would pay attention to me like this." This thought should have been my red flag to look for the way of escape and get the heck out of Dodge, but like I said earlier, I am a slow learner sometimes.

I didn't take the way of escape and I allowed the temptation and flirtation with sin to continue. The young woman and I started having lunch together. I convinced myself that it was harmless because nothing physical was happening. Then I started venting to her about the situation with my wife (that is another very bad idea, but that is a topic for a different book). Before I knew it, I had developed an inappropriate relationship with this woman emotionally, one that would get way too close for comfort. I crossed a lot of lines! The situation should have never made it to that point. As a result, I had to quit my job; a job that I really enjoyed. That was my only way of escape at that point because I allowed the temptation to fester for so long. It was so far along in the process that I had to do something drastic to overcome the temptation.

It was through that situation that I really learned how temptation and sin works. I was led away by my desire for a type of attention I felt I was not getting at home. I allowed myself to be convinced that I was justified in feeling the way I felt and that I deserved the attention I was getting from the young woman. I spent my time venting to the young woman instead of talking to my wife. God gave me a way of escape several times. Each time I chose my path over His. Each way of escape came with a higher price tag. Eventually, it cost me my job. Even worse, I had yet to tell my wife which meant I still faced the possibility of losing her. The worst part of all of this was the hurt I saw in her eyes when I confessed.

The longer we allow temptation to fester, the closer we get to sin. The closer we get to sin, the more we hurt ourselves and the people we love. In addition to the hurt we cause, the longer temptation festers the more increasingly difficult it becomes to avoid the act of sin. I am thankful for a forgiving wife and a merciful, forgiving heavenly Father.

Unaddressed temptation will give birth to sin. Sin, when it is born, will bring forth death, as James 1:15 says. Death, spiritual death, is separation from God. In the section, "Does Your Temple Match God's Blueprint?" we talked about the fact that we are the temple of God because the Holy Spirit dwells inside of us. You may be wondering how we can experience separation from God if the Holy Spirit lives in us? The Holy Spirit is our life giving force. Sin causes us to become malnourished Christians. Malnourishment leads to ineffectiveness. We become ineffective in our ability to defend against the fiery darts of the enemy. We become ineffective in our prayer lives. Our growth becomes stunted and we cease to mature as Christians. We become separated from God's will for our lives.

Since a Christian cannot lose his or her salvation, we cannot be totally separated from God, but we should not take that for granted. In Romans 6:1, the Apostle Paul says it this way: *"Shall we continue in sin that grace may abound? Certainly not! How*

Consensual Christianity

shall we who died to sin live any longer in it?" One of the many roles of the Holy Spirit in our lives is to convict us of sin and draw us to repentance. If you are a Christian, the Holy Spirit lives in you and He will convict you of sin until you repent! He will not allow your sin to go unchecked because it offends Him. Hebrews 12:5-6 explains this to us, *"My son, do not despise the chastening of the Lord, nor be discouraged when you are rebuked by Him: for whom the Lord loves He chastens, and scourges every son whom He receives."*

Let me challenge you; if you find yourself at the onset of temptation, speak God's word. If you find yourself in the midst of temptation, flee from it as fast and as far as you can. Do not allow it to fester. Learn from my mistake… nothing good ever comes out of allowing temptation to fester. If you've allowed your temptation to fester and now find yourself in the midst of sin, confess and repent. Don't let one sin become many sins by trying to cover it up. Unaddressed temptation will lead to sin. Unrepentant sin will lead to separation from God and from God's will. It will eventually render us ineffective. We cannot grow and mature as Christians if we give place to sin in our lives. Sin is our number one hindrance.

Then Jesus said to His disciples, "If anyone desires to come after Me, let him deny himself, and take up his cross, and follow Me. For whoever desires to save his life will lose it, but whoever loses his life for My sake will find it. For what profit is it to a man if he gains the whole world, and loses his own soul? Or what shall a man give in exchange for his soul?[43]

---

43   Matthew 16:24-26, NKJV

Your Spiritual Identity:

One of the most beautiful side effects of having a real relationship with God is the realization of your identity in Christ. Take notice of the way I worded that, "your identity in Christ." The Apostle Paul talked about this new identity quite frequently. Two passages of Scripture in particular come to mind. The first is 2 Corinthians 5:17. "Therefore, if anyone is in Christ, he is a new creation; old things have passed away; behold, all things have become new. The second scripture is Romans 8:1, "There is now no condemnation to those who are in Christ Jesus, who do not walk according to the flesh but according to the Spirit. Based on these Scriptures we can determine that once we are in Christ we are no longer the same old sinful man or woman that we used to be. Prior to being in Christ, your sin nature ruled and reigned in your life. Once you are in Christ, you are set free and have become a new creature. Romans 8:1 provides us with yet another beautiful piece and that is the primary characteristic of those who are in Christ; they do not walk according to the flesh but according to the Spirit. We talk about this more in a later chapter so I am not going to go into too much detail about that here.

Our identity in Christ is that of one who walks according to the Spirit of God, one who produces fruit for God's kingdom, one who has peace instead of despair, joy instead of sorrow, love instead of hate and fear. There is one thing that hinders our relationship and thus clouds our identity in Christ and that is sin. Sin separates us from God; it keeps us from following His will and causes us to stumble. Separation from God is spiritual death as He is the one who gives us life through His Holy Spirit. Romans 8:11 tells us that the same Spirit that raised Jesus from the dead now dwells in us and gives life (spiritual life) to our mortal bodies. We are truly alive in Christ.

I will be honest and admit that I have at times allowed sin and doubt to hinder my relationship with God. I have struggled with some serious, at times debilitating, sins that have kept me from experiencing God the way He desires for me to experience Him. Don't allow sin to keep you from God, and don't allow doubt to keep you from trusting Him. The Bible tells us that if we confess our sins, God is faithful and just to forgive us and to cleanse us of all unrighteousness. He is faithful even when we are not. Confess your sins and allow Him to cleanse you. We will all be tempted and at times we will fail. Isn't it good to know that God never fails?

Know who you are in Christ! You are more than a conqueror. You are a joint heir to the kingdom of God. You are a child of God. You are a royal priesthood. You are the redeemed of the Lord, and as the Psalmist so wonderfully stated, let all of the redeemed of the Lord say so... I AM REDEEMED! You are not your sin nor are not your' past. You are a child of Almighty God. Live like you believe that you are victorious in Christ.

6

Where Do We Go From Here?

For we are His workmanship, created in Christ Jesus for good works, which God prepared beforehand that we should walk in them.

Ephesians 2:10

Chapter 6

Each and every relationship is different. I remember
when my wife and I got married. One of the requirements
our pastor gave us, prior to marrying us, was to go through
premarital counseling. During our premarital counseling, our
pastor gave us a book called *Saving Your Marriage before It Starts:
Seven Questions to Ask Before and After You Marry* by Dr. Les Parrott
and Dr. Leslie Parrott. There are accompanying workbooks for
men and women, which we found to be very helpful. I highly
recommend this book to those of you who are either engaged or
considering marriage. It is a great resource, one that my wife and
I still refer back to it from time to time to give advice to others or
just to remember the things we discussed prior to marriage. The
purpose of the book, and the premarital counseling sessions,
was to cause us to consider things that we may be overlooking;
things we may have assumed would just work themselves out.

We discussed a lot of little things like who would be
responsible for paying the bills, who would discipline the children,
who would initiate sex, who would do the dishes, and so on and
so forth. At the time I thought it was tedious but after being
married for just a short time I realized how critical discussing
those things beforehand actually was in our relationship.

Let me give you an example. I grew up in a house where
my mom managed the family finances. My wife, on the other
hand, grew up in a home where her dad managed the family
finances. If we did not discuss this prior to marriage, I would
have assumed she was going to manage the finances and she
would have assumed I would do it since that is what our prior

115

experiences dictated. As you can imagine, that could have created some issues. Well, this section of the book covers some of the things we may overlook in our relationship with God; things we may assume would just work themselves out.

So now what? Where do we begin this journey? Christianity is a lifestyle not a religion; as a result, there are principles that help us maintain a healthy lifestyle. Just as you must follow certain principles to maintain a healthy body, you must follow certain principles to maintain a healthy spirit. If you want to live the lifestyle of an athlete, you cannot fill yourself with junk food. To the contrary, you must be cautious about the foods you eat, you must exercise and pay proper attention to your physical body. Well, we are going to discuss some principles that, if followed, will help you achieve God's best in your life.

The principles we are going to discuss in this section are stewardship, forgiveness, and love. It is important that we understand these principles and the way they relate to God's will for us. All too often, believers want to experience being in God's will without following the principles laid out in His word. Let me be the one to tell you: "It doesn't work that way!" God is our faithful Father and He promises to protect and provide for us, but just like every Father, He has some expectations for us. It is our responsibility to be obedient to His word and live out His principles in our daily lives. The good news is that He gives us the grace we need to be successful and the strength to endure. His strength truly is perfected in our weakness. These three topics: stewardship, forgiveness, and love may seem trivial in a sense. We know that, as Christians, we are to love others, but what does that really look like lived out on a daily basis? We know that we are supposed to forgive others, but how do we forgive those who have deeply hurt us and left us with scars? Likewise, we know that we should take care of all that God has given us, but what does that include and how do I demonstrate good stewardship? Knowing these things and living these things are two completely different things. We are going to start with stewardship, learning to manage all that God has given us in a way that demonstrates our obedience to Him and ultimately glorifies Him.

Stewardship

Stewardship is the act of being a steward. What does it mean to be a steward? According to the dictionary, a steward is one employed in a large household or estate to manage domestic concerns. Think about that, God has chosen us to manage the concerns of His estate. He has given us access to all that is His and He expects us to manage it properly. So what are the things that He has given us stewardship over? Most people associate stewardship with financial resources but it is much more than that. James 1:16-17 says, *"Do not be deceived, my beloved brethren. Every good and perfect gift is from above and comes down from the Father of lights, with whom there is no variation or shadow of turning."* In other words, every good thing we have comes from God and He does not vary; He does not change His mind. It is these "good and perfect gifts" that we are to be good stewards of. One of my

117

favorite scriptures is Numbers 23:19; *"God is not a man that He should lie nor the son of man that He should change His mind. Has He said and will He not do? Has He spoken and will He not make it good?"* When God gives you something, He does not change His mind and take it back, the gift is always there. It is we who choose to walk away; we are the ones who choose to live in the fullness of His gift or to refuse it.

So what are these "good and perfect gifts?" These gifts include time (our lifespan), relationships (family, friends, and neighbors), financial resources, personal gifts and talents, and our bodies (His temple). Every day we are given opportunities to exercise our stewardship and demonstrate our ability to properly manage His concerns. You may wonder what that looks like in action. The Apostle Paul talks to us about being good stewards of our time in Ephesians 5:16 when he says, "Redeeming the time, because the days are evil." Redeeming the time means "making the most of it." We are to spend our time on the things that matter to God and put it to good use, not waste it on selfish or unfruitful things. Does that mean there is no time for fun? Absolutely not, but what is it that you consider fun? Spending time with family and friends can be very fun and a good use of time as you are able to build those relationships while being an example of a godly man or woman. I don't spend every minute of every day reading the Bible or in church. I love playing with my kids and what a wonderful opportunity to show them how they can relate to their heavenly Father by being a loving earthly father. The same principle applies to spending time with friends.

You can have a good time with friends and be a witness without ever mentioning the Bible. Your actions speak much louder than your words ever could. In the process, you are being a good steward of your time and relationships. Your actions are your greatest witness. Being a Christian doesn't mean you have to live a boring life. To the contrary, we should be the most exciting people to be around because we have the joy of the Lord.

Jesus tells us how to be a good steward of the interactions we have with others on a daily basis. Matthew 5:14-16 says, *"You are the light of the world. A city that is set on a hill cannot be hid. Neither do men light a candle, and put it under a bushel, but on a candlestick and it gives light to all that are in the house. Let your light so shine before men, that they may see your good works, and glorify your Father which is in heaven."* We demonstrate our stewardship of relationships by allowing our light to shine. What does that mean though? How do we let our light shine? It goes back to our actions. I have spoken with many individuals who were once part of a local church but decided to walk away. It amazes me how many choose to refuse God based on the actions of another person. When you proclaim to be a Christian it is important that your lifestyle match your proclamation. Our lifestyle is our light. We are either individual examples of a life dedicated to Christ or examples of a life in need of Christ. The life of a Christian is powered by the Holy Spirit, by studying God's word, and by spending time with God in prayer. The less you spend time with God, the lower your power level will be. The lower your power level is, the dimmer your light will be. Every interaction you have is an opportunity to make a positive or negative impact on someone. What impact do you have on the people around you? When people look at you, what do they see? Do they see a life dedicated to Christ and following in His footsteps or a life of hypocrisy? Remember, you are a child of God and a representative of His family.

So far, we have discussed outward stewardship or stewardship as it pertains to others. Now let's take a look at inward stewardship; stewardship of the things that directly affect us. Let's start with the stewardship of our bodies. I often get strange looks when I talk about this because it is something that is not normally discussed. God gives us these earthly bodies as a vessel to accomplish the tasks He has preordained for us. So how can we accomplish our preordained tasks if our bodies are falling apart, riddled with sickness and disease because of our poor management? I am not referring to individuals who have diseases like cancer at no fault of their own. My prayers go out for those individuals and their families. I am referring to people who, due to poor eating habits and lack of exercise, find themselves suffering from obesity and other related illnesses. I was one of those individuals for a number of years. How can we be effective for the kingdom of God if we are constantly bed ridden due to sickness that stems from our poor health choices? We need to be good stewards of the body that God has given us and maximize its potential for His kingdom. Does that mean we will not get sick? No, but it does mean that we should not be the source of our own sickness. This not only applies to sickness related to obesity but also to sickness as a result of drug and alcohol abuse. Please don't take this the wrong way. There are some individuals with very strong addictions to drugs, alcohol, and eating. Addictions that are too powerful for us to overcome on our own but it is our responsibility to seek God, find help in a time of need, and make every effort to overcome these things. How silly would I sound praying for God to help me lose weight while shoving a box of doughnuts in my mouth? Pretty silly, right, but that is what we do so often. We pray for deliverance from issues we are causing. God made us stewards over our bodies, it is our duty to maintain them the best we possibly can and to trust Him for the things we cannot do.

Another opportunity for us to demonstrate our inward stewardship is with our financial resources. The reason I grouped finances in the "inward stewardship" category is because our use of money usually reflects the condition of our heart. God gives us the resources we need to live and accomplish the things He has called us to do. It is our responsibility to properly manage these resources. A big part of being a faithful steward of the money God gives us is in being a generous giver. Pay attention to the wording of the previous sentence: "the money God gives us." Earlier, James 1:17 told us that *every good and perfect gift comes down from the Father of lights.* When we give out of obedience to what God has asked, we are not giving God part of our income; we are giving back to Him what is rightfully His. He gives us 100% of all we have with the understanding that we will be generous when He asks us to give.

Many of us assume that our monetary resources do not

Consensual Christianity

come from God but rather are a product of us using our natural gifts, talents, and abilities. Let me ask a question; where do our natural gifts, talents, and abilities come from? We certainly did not give these things to ourselves. God gives us our gifts, talents, and abilities as a means to do what He has designed us to do. He allows us to use them as a means to provide for our families but He also expects us to use them and/or the influence we gain as a result of them for His kingdom. In high school, I played on the varsity basketball team. I remember standing in the gym one day and telling my friend, "This is my sanctuary." He looked at me like I was crazy but I believed that I was worshipping God by using the ability that God gave me to the full. I was determined to give it my all and do the best I could while maintaining an attitude that glorified Him. A good litmus test for the way you use your gifts and talents is to ask yourself, "who or what am I trying to benefit by doing this? Myself or the Kingdom of God?" Hopefully you think I have a gift for writing; if not I apologize that you have had to suffer through so much of the book. I could choose to use that gift as a means to make money and only write books that would sell in great quantities. That usually means lots of sex and violence, get rich quick schemes, or the next great self-help craze, or I could choose to write material that glorifies God and helps to advance the Gospel. The gift is the same but I determine how I use it. The real question is whether you are more concerned with achieving earthly rewards or heavenly ones.

The principle of stewardship is essential to living a

fruitful life as a Christian. We must properly manage our Father's concerns here on earth. He promises to reward us in Heaven if we take proper care of the things He has asked us to be good stewards over here on earth. Jesus gives us the perfect depiction of this in the parable of the talents.[44] I want to encourage you to take some time to read it. It is a wonderful, practical lesson given by our great Teacher.

Forgiveness

As Christians, we have all experienced forgiveness first hand as God accepted the perfect sacrifice (Jesus) and forgave us of our sins when we accepted His free gift of salvation. What a glorious experience! When you accepted the gift of salvation, Jesus paid your sin debt in full. Every sin you committed up to that point was cleared off of your account. In addition, the sins you commit after that can be removed if you confess them to the Father and ask for forgiveness. 1 John 1:9 says, *"If we confess our sins, He is faithful and just to forgive us our sins and to cleanse us from all unrighteousness."* As Christians, we know how to receive forgiveness but do we know how to truly give it? How do you forgive the people who have wronged you and caused you pain? How do you forgive the spouse that cheated on you? How do you forgive the relative that abused you as a child? How do you forgive the employer that treated you wrongly or the friend that betrayed you? In Isaiah 43:25, God tells us, *"I, even I, am he that blots out your transgressions for my own sake, and will not remember your*

---

44   Matthew 25:14-30, NKJV

sins." So, if God can forgive and forget, why can't we?

Well, if you believe that God is omniscient and you believe Psalm 139:16, *"Your eyes saw my unformed substance; in your book were written, every one of them, the days that were formed for me, when as yet there was none of them;"* then you will also believe that God does not actually forget our sins. To say that He knows all yet forgets something is counterintuitive. Yet, that's what we think He means when He says, "I will not remember your sins." We assume we are to do the same so we say we should "forgive and forget." I think we need to change our perspective on that and stop trying to "forgive and forget" and start trying to "forgive and no longer hold accountable." If you have ever been deeply hurt by someone, you know that it is impossible to forget what has happened but we can, once we choose to forgive them, choose to no longer hold them accountable for what they have done.

Has someone ever done something that hurt you and asked for forgiveness? Did you forgive them? Once you did, did you continue on with the relationship? Did that person ever mess up again? If so, did you only hold them accountable for their new mistake or did you also bring up the ones you had already "forgiven" them for? I know the answer to that question many times in my own life. So now I have to ask myself a new question. What if that was the way God operated? What if I sinned today and He decided to hold me accountable for today's sin and every other sin I committed in the past, even though He said those sins were forgiven? Would there be any hope of salvation? What would that say about the God we serve? What does that say about you and me when we do it?

Matthew 6:9-13, also known as "The Lord's Prayer" is an example of how we ought to pray:

"Our Father in heaven, hallowed be your name. Your kingdom come, Your will be done on earth as it is in heaven. Give us this day our daily bread and forgive us our trespasses (sins) as we forgive those who trespass against us. Lead us not into temptation but deliver us from the evil one. For Yours is the kingdom and the power and the glory forever. Amen."

What a powerful prayer: a prayer for provision, protection, and forgiveness. A prayer of adoration and exaltation; what a powerful prayer! I will not go in to too much detail about the Lord's prayer other than to say that Jesus teaches us how to ask for forgiveness, *"and forgive us our trespasses as we forgive those who trespass against us."* Pay close attention to the word "As" in the middle of that sentence. The word "As" in the middle of the statement implies a simultaneous act. This is further explained if you read the two verses following the prayer. Matthew 6:14-15, *"For if you forgive men their trespasses, your heavenly Father will also forgive you. But if you do not forgive men their trespasses, neither will your Father forgive your trespasses."*

Does that really say that if I don't forgive others God will not forgive me? Yes, it does! Forgiving others is that important. So important that Jesus clearly states, if we don't do it, we will not be forgiven either. He also provides us a wonderful picture of this in Matthew 18:23-35:

Consensual Christianity

"Therefore is the kingdom of heaven likened to a certain king, which would take account of his servants. And when he had begun to reckon, one was brought to him, which owed him ten thousand talents. But for as much as he had not to pay, his lord commanded him to be sold, and his wife, and children, and all that he had, and payment to be made. The servant therefore fell down, and worshipped him, saying, Lord, have patience with me, and I will pay you all. Then the lord of that servant was moved with compassion, and loosed him, and forgave him the debt. But the same servant went out, and found one of his fellow servants, which owed him an hundred pence: and he laid hands on him, and took him by the throat, saying, Pay me that you owe. And his fellow servant fell down at his feet, and sought him, saying, Have patience with me, and I will pay you all. And he would not: but went and cast him into prison, till he should pay the debt. So when his fellow servants saw what was done, they were very sorry, and came and told to their lord all that was done. Then his lord, after that he had called him, said to him, O you wicked servant, I forgave you all that debt, because you desired me: Should not you also have had compassion on your fellow servant, even as I had pity on you? And his lord was wroth, and delivered him to the tormentors, till he should pay all that was due to him. So likewise shall my heavenly Father do also to you, if you from your hearts forgive not everyone his brother their trespasses."

God is a righteous judge. There will come a day when the wicked will be judged in accordance with their actions. If you want to be truly forgiven, you must first truly forgive. Think about all that God has forgiven you for, how much more should we offer true forgiveness to those who have wronged us.

Love

In the first edition of *Consensual Christianity*, I took a more academic approach to the topic of *love*, looking at the Greek words used in the New Testament that we translate as *love*. In this, the second edition, I want to take a little different approach. I do believe that understanding the differences between the words used in the original Biblical text is important, especially from the standpoint of studying and comprehending the Bible. However, after a lot of study and meditating on God's word, I have come to the conclusion that simply defining the different Greek words is not enough. We have to look at love in light of its application to fully understand what it is and what God expects of us.

In case you had not noticed, I like to use examples from my personal experience, especially my marriage, because it is an easy way for me to draw correlations between Biblical principles and real life application. The English language can be very confusing because we tend to ascribe multiple meanings to singular words. When that is combined with the use of slang and dialect, we can run into a very complicated issue. It can be difficult to decipher the true meaning of some words, especially those attached to our emotions, because they can be clouded by our experiences. You have heard the old saying, "Hindsight is 20/20," right? Well, in hindsight, I realize that I have used the word "love" in the wrong context quite frequently in my life. There have been times where I should have said, "I really like you," instead of "I love you." There have also been some times where my emotions where much closer to lust than love, yet

Consensual Christianity

love was used to justify my lusts. I know I am not the only guilty party.

The inherent confusion in our language has given me an appreciation for other languages. New Testament Greek, for instance, uses three primary words that we translate as love: *Agap'e*, *Agapao*, and *Phileo*. There is a fourth, fairly common word for *love* in the Greek, *eros*, but it is not readily used in the Bible. *Eros* is used to denote love that has a desire to possess, i.e. I love something therefore I want to own it.[45] It is often used in a negative connotation. The three primary words: *agap'e*, *agapao*, and *phileo* are used numerous times in the New Testament. Agap'e and Agapao are similar in meaning. *Agap'e* is a noun, used to denote love in the form of benevolence. We often refer to agap'e as "unconditional love," but a better interpretation would be "unmerited love."[46] *Agapao* is the verb form of *agap'e* and typically means to love in a social or moral sense.[47] In both cases, love is unmerited and given out of a sense of duty or principle. *Phileo* is usually indicative of brotherly love, a feelings based, merited, emotional type of love.[48] *Phileo*, unlike *agap'e* or *agapao* can be won or lost. To illustrate this, we are going to view these words in a passage of Scripture, John 15: 9-19. In this passage, Jesus is talking to His disciples, just prior to His betrayal

---

45   Elwell, Walter A. (2001). Evangelical Dictionary of Theology: Second Edition. Grand Rapids, MI: Baker Publishing Group

46   Strong, J. (1995). *The New Strong's Exhaustive Concordance of the Bible.* Nashville, TN: Thomas Nelson Publishers

47   Strong, J. *Strong's Exhaustive Concordance.*

48   Strong, J. *Strong's Exhaustive Concordance.*

and crucifixion. Each time the word *love* is used in the Scripture, I will give you the corresponding Greek word in parenthesis.

⁹As the Father loved Me, I also have loved you; abide in My love (Agap'e). If you keep My commandments you will abide in My love (Agap'e), just as I have kept My Father's commandments and I abide in His love (Agap'e). ¹² This is my commandment, that you love (Agapao) one another as I have loved you. ¹³Greater love (Agap'e) has no one than this, than to lay down one's life for his friends. ¹⁷These things I command you, that you love (Agapao) one another. ¹⁹If you were of the world, the world would love (Phileo) its own. Yet because you are not of the world, but I chose you out of the world, therefore the world hates you.

In the interest of time and space, I skipped the verses that did not contain the word *love*. If we view the words in light of whether or not they are merited, it helps us to understand the difference and the true meaning of the Scripture. Jesus' love for us is unmerited. He expects our love for one another to be unmerited as well. This is the same type of love referenced in 1 Corinthians 13:4-8, unmerited, benevolent love. Viewing John 15:9-19 also helps us understand the similarity between *agap'e* and *agapao*. It is easy to see agap'e being used as a noun and *agapao* used as a verb. The one use of the word *phileo* also stands out. The world's love of its own is merit based love, it has to be earned and can be lost... it has a "what have you done for me lately" quality.

When God calls for us to love one another, to love Him,

to love our spouses and our kids, and to love our neighbors, it is always an unmerited, unwarranted type of love. All too often, we view our relationships through the eyes of merit and, consequently, our relationships often fall short. Perhaps, this explains why so many marriages end in divorce. Why two people who seemed so in love at one point can no longer stand the sight of one another. Perhaps their love was merit based instead of unmerited. God's holiness, righteousness, and unmerited love for us are the reasons He offered us reconciliation in Christ. It was for those reasons that He sent His only Son to die for our sins. If God's love toward us was merit based, only Christ could have earned His love; we would all be subjected to His wrath.

When I think about love, it helps me to utilize the two aforementioned categories. If I am doing something out of love, but that love is expecting something in return, it is merit based and has the potential to falling short and not last. If my acts are unmerited acts of benevolence, then I know they will have a lasting impact. Matthew 5:46 ask us the most poignant question on this topic: *"For if you love those who love you, what reward have you?* I am of the opinion that the majority of the time we use the word love, we are referring to the merit based, emotional type of love. This is why we talk about falling in and out of love so often. True love, unmerited love, is not something that can be fallen in and out of. It is an inherent quality, much like the love of a parent for a child.

Prayer

For me personally, the single most difficult area of relating to God is prayer. I don't know why I have struggled with it so much. Perhaps I am not struggling as much as I think I am; maybe I have unfairly compared myself to other believers. I just know that I always feel like I am either doing it wrong or not doing it enough. I realized long ago that I am not one who can pray for hours at a time. I applaud those who can do that. My prayers are usually more of the 5 to 10 minute variety. I can do praise and worship for hours. I can even read my Bible for long periods of time because I love to study, but prayer just doesn't come naturally for me. I used to really beat myself up over this because I felt it meant I was falling short in some way. Thankfully, the Holy Spirit showed me the error in my thinking and helped me gain a better understanding of what it means to have a good prayer life.

I am somewhat of an introvert, which is pretty weird seeing how I love to teach and have no problem speaking in front of large crowds of people. Being an introvert does not make me shy; it just means that I prefer to be low key whenever possible. I am not much of a talker outside of teaching. Remember how I told you that we will all connect with God in different ways because He created us as unique individuals. Well, my personality has had a direct impact on the way I connect to God and the way I pray. The Holy Spirit showed me, through His word, how to pray effectively even though I don't pray for hours at a time. Before I dive into this, let me state a few things.

131

Consensual Christianity

First, don't make the mistake I did of comparing yourself to others. God is more concerned with the quality of our prayer life than the quantity. That is also true for praise and worship and reading the Bible. Assuming that we have to spend a specific amount of time in each to hear from God is limiting God and placing unnecessary restrictions on us. The important thing is to ensure that each is a part of our lives and to do them in the most authentic fashion, being true to who God made us to be, adhering to His word, and respecting His holiness. Secondly, prayer is not a mystical thing like a séance or some strange ritual. It is a time of conversation with our Heavenly Father. There is not a magic set of words to get you the results we are looking for. God does, however, concern Himself with the purpose or motivation behind our prayers as we see in James 4:2-3: *"You lust and do not have. You murder and covet and cannot obtain. You fight and war, yet you do not have because you do not ask. You ask and do not receive, because you ask amiss, that you may spend it on your pleasures."* Lastly, I used to assume that prayer, praise and worship, and reading the Bible were independent of one another. However, I now understand that the three usually work together in our lives. God uses all of them to talk with us, teach and instruct us, and to guide us. They are all times of growth and refreshing for us. We talked about this briefly in "How Do You Connect to God." Just remember that each of us is unique and will connect to Him in different ways. We should work on strengthening our areas of weakness; however, the weakness should not be our focus. Connecting with God should be our focus.

Chapter 6

You may be like I was and question why you need to tell God what is going on in your life. After all, He is God and He knows everything, right? That is true. He is God and He does know all but God is a gentleman and He will not intrude in your life. We invite Him in by sharing our heart with Him. Two verses in Scripture are indicative of this; Philippians 4:6 and 1 Peter 5:7. Philippians 4:6 says, *"Be anxious for nothing; but in everything by prayer and supplication with thanksgiving let your requests be made known to God."* 1 Peter 5:7 says; *"Cast all your cares on him; for he cares for you."* What picture is painted in your mind by these verses? For me, they paint a picture of my loving heavenly Father longing to care for me, longing to get involved in my life; all I need to do is invite Him in. Many people question whether or not an omnipotent God is concerned with lowly human beings. According to Philippians 4:6 and 1 Peter 5:7, He is. God cares for you and He promises to never leave you nor forsake you.

Bringing our needs and worries to God in prayer is part of the reason we pray but it is not the only reason we pray. Prayer is not a time for grocery listing all of our requests or reading a wish list like a child would on Santa's lap, instead, it truly is a time of conversation. Jesus instructed the disciples to pray in this manner:

"Our Father, who art in heaven, hallowed be thy name. Thy kingdom come, thy will be done on earth as it is in heaven. Give us this day our daily bread and forgive us our trespasses as we forgive those who trespass against us. Lead us not into temptation but deliver us from the evil one. For thine is the

Consensual Christianity

kingdom, the power and the glory forever and ever. Amen.[49]

Does that mean that we are to repeat this prayer each and every time we pray? I don't believe so, although there is nothing wrong with including it in your daily prayers. I believe that Jesus was giving us an example of things to include in our prayer. Not a magical formula, but more of a guide. Prayer, like any conversation, will be different for each of us because we are all unique individuals with our own set of experiences, habits, and relating techniques.

Praise. Jesus started the prayer by saying "Our Father in heaven, hallowed be thy name." The word "hallowed" means "holy or consecrated, set apart." Jesus was saying that God's name is holy, deserving of respect and reverence. He was telling us that we must first acknowledge who we are praying to with the respect and honor that is due to our heavenly Father. Praise is an essential part of prayer. The dictionary defines praise as "to glorify, especially by the attribution of perfections." Praise is our way of showing God that we believe in Him, even in the midst of our trouble.

Submitting to God's authority. The second line in the Lord's Prayer is, *"Thy kingdom come, thy will be done on earth as it is in heaven."* Jesus was telling us to acknowledge God's sovereignty and pray that God's will be done here on earth the same way it is in heaven. Jesus demonstrated this again in His personal prayer life. Matthew 26:39 says, *"And he went a little farther, and fell on his*

---

49   Matthew 6:9-13, NKJV

face, and prayed, saying, O my Father, if it be possible, let this cup pass from me: nevertheless not as I will, but as you will." This is part of the prayer Jesus prayed before He was betrayed as He knew His time had come and He would have to suffer greatly. Submitting to God's authority can be difficult because it can require sacrifice on our part. Jesus knew that His sacrifice would cost His life. Thankfully, He stayed committed to the Father's will even to the point of death because He also knew the promises and the joy that awaited Him. He knew that His pain would be temporary and well worth the eternal joy He would receive as a result.

Provision. "Give us this day our daily bread." This is a prayer for provision; asking God to provide for our needs. We discussed casting our care and worry upon God and allowing Him to show His love and care for us previously but I want you to notice how short this portion of the prayer actually is. Matthew 6:25-33 says:

Therefore I say to you, Take no thought for your life, what you shall eat, or what you shall drink; nor yet for your body, what you shall put on. Is not the life more than meat, and the body than raiment? Behold the fowls of the air: for they sow not, neither do they reap, nor gather into barns; yet your heavenly Father feeds them. Are you not much better than they? Which of you by taking thought can add one cubit to his stature? And why take you thought for raiment? Consider the lilies of the field, how they grow; they toil not, neither do they spin: And yet I say to you, That even Solomon in all his glory was not arrayed like one of these. Why, if God so clothe the grass of the field, which today is, and tomorrow is cast into the oven, shall he not

Consensual Christianity

much more clothe you, O you of little faith? Therefore take no thought, saying, What shall we eat? or, What shall we drink? or, Wherewithal shall we be clothed? (For after all these things do the Gentiles seek:) for your heavenly Father knows that you have need of all these things. But seek you first the kingdom of God, and his righteousness; and all these things shall be added to you."

The message here is to focus on the things of God and let Him take care of the things that concern you. Remember, there is a big difference between needs and wants. God is our heavenly Father, not our magical genie. He promises to provide for all of our needs but He does NOT tell us that He will grant all of our wishes.

Forgiveness. We discussed this in great detail in a previous chapter. Just remember to ask forgiveness for the sins you have committed and be forgiving to others. This is a great time in prayer to be accountable for the actions of the day. This actually will help you not only learn to forgive as you are forgiven but also to be a good steward of the time God has given you. Trust me when I tell you that giving an account to God for the things you have done will help keep you on the right path. Each time you are faced with a temptation or in a bad situation, think to yourself, "I am going to give a detailed account of this to God; do I really want to explain this to my heavenly Father?" It keeps me in line and I believe it will help you also.

Trusting God to do what He said He will do. God wants to know that we trust in His sovereignty and His promises.

He wants to know that we believe in Him and that we know He is a rewarder of those who diligently seek Him. Jesus ended the prayer by saying, "For thine (yours) is the Kingdom, the power and the glory forever and ever." He was acknowledging that God is in control. He was acknowledging the fact that God has the power and authority to do all things according to His will and purpose; without Him, we are powerless to do anything. How do we demonstrate our trust in His sovereignty? We let go and let Him take control. Remember, when we pray about our needs and concerns, we are giving God an invitation into our circumstances. The best thing we can do is get out of the way and let Him do what only He can. Does that mean we stop praying about it? No, but it does mean that we stop trying to fix it ourselves. It is ok to pray about something multiple times. Just remember to stay focused on God and not the problem.

While there is not a magical "bippety boppety boo" we can say to get results, we can stand firm on the word of God and know that He is always true to His word. Quoting Scripture in your prayers is a great tool if you don't know exactly what to say. It builds your faith and shows that you know the principles you are standing on. Prayer should be a part of each and every day of your life; after all, it is a conversation with our Father. Don't allow the enemy to trick you into believing that God is not concerned with you. His word says that He is. Also, don't fall into the belief that prayer is all about making petitions and requests of God. While they are a part of prayer, they alone are not prayer. There is so much more to prayer than we often

Consensual Christianity

assume. Thank you Jesus for painting such a beautiful picture of prayer and demonstrating it in Your life. Spend some time with the Lord in prayer. He longs to hear from you and loves your conversation.

Basic Training:

There are some basic essentials that every Christian should have a proper grasp of: love, forgiveness and prayer. Why these three? One is the primary characteristic of our Heavenly Father. The second is what allows us to be reconciled to Him and in relationship with Him, and the third is our primary means of communicating with Him. Throughout my time as a Christian, I have had to learn what it really means to love others, especially those who are not easy to love. As we examine the life of Jesus, we see that He reached out to those who were considered untouchable by society, such as those stricken with leprosy. We also see that He took time to minister to those who were desperately trapped in sin like the adulterous woman. Jesus, through His life and ministry, shows us how to love others.

Did you know it is possible to hate sin yet still love sinners? Jesus is proof. He died to free us from the penalty of sin. He hated sin so much that He allowed Himself to be nailed to the Cross so He could defeat its power. Yet, He loved sinners. Mark 6:34 says that Jesus, when He saw the crowds, was moved with compassion because they were as sheep not having a shepherd. Now we know Jesus is the Good Shepherd and the Good Shepherd saw a crowd of sheep, bound by sin, and He

138

was so moved with compassion because His heart's desire was to guide them and to protect them like a shepherd does his flock.

Learning to love others the way Jesus loves others will help you forgive others. Forgiveness is one of those things that seem pretty easy to do on paper yet it is very difficult to do in reality. Trust me, I know. However, what I also know is that unforgiveness only hurts you. For years, I refused to forgive those who wronged me as a child. That unforgiveness caused a root of bitterness to grow in my heart that opened the doors of sin in my life. If you think back to the book's intro, you will remember that I really struggled with anxiety and depression, and eventually tried to kill myself. The root of all of that was the bitterness and unforgiveness that I held on to in my heart.

I would like to challenge you, take time to search your heart. Determine if there is someone you have not been able to forgive and, if so, pray for God's help. Ask Jesus to help you to forgive just as He did as He said "Father forgive them, for they know not what they do." We often hold on to unforgiveness because we assume the person hurt us on purpose. The truth of the matter is that if the person is not a Christian, they are living under the bondage of sin and being led by their sin nature. That does not excuse their actions but it does explain their actions. Humans, apart from Christ, are selfish, proud, deceitful, and wicked; some more so than others. Your forgiveness might just be the catalyst that God uses to bring that person to Himself. Forgive! Allow God to heal your hurts and to use you as a living witness of His mercy in the midst of a lost and dying world.

Consensual Christianity

7

Let's Get Started!

Finally my brethren, be strong in the Lord and in the power of His might. Put on the whole armor of God, that you may be able to stand against the wiles of the devil.

Ephesians 6:10-11

Consensual Christianity

There is something beautiful about the vibrancy and exuberance of a new believer; their joyful innocence having not been mired by legalism and years of spiritual battle. I love to watch them as the lift their hands in surrender to their Savior. They look so free. Psalm 51:10-13 seems to embody what they are experiencing:

Create in me a clean heart, O God. And renew a steadfast spirit within me. Do not cast me away from Your presence, and do not take Your Holy Spirit from me. Restore to me the joy of Your salvation, and uphold me by Your generous Spirit. Then I will teach transgressors Your ways, and sinners shall be converted to You.

A clean heart is very liberating. The heavy weight from years of sin being completely removed brings great joy and a new passion for life. You can't help but tell everyone you come into contact with. I have also noticed that this period seems to wane in many, myself included. Why does this youthful exuberance leave us? Why do we seem to fall into the doldrums of life? Why can we not seem to maintain the joy of salvation in our lives? There are several reasons. First, when we accept Christ, we become an enemy to Satan. Satan will do his best to distract and destroy us. As Jesus said, *"The thief has come to steal, kill, and destroy, but I have come that you may have life and have it more abundantly"* (John 10:10). Second, we forget about our first love and place our focus on other things. When we get saved, we are consumed with getting to know God, reading His word, and praising Him for all He has done and is doing in our lives. As time goes on, our priorities often change. Lastly, the rough times lead us to periods of renewing. Psalm 51:10-13 is part of the prayer David prayed after he committed adultery with Bathsheba and had her husband, Uriah, killed. David, after his terrible acts, was praying for newness and restoration. He wanted to once again experience the joy of salvation, the youthful exuberance of being set free from bondage. Our minds need to be renewed daily. Romans 12:2 says it this way: *"Do not be conformed to this world, but be transformed by the renewing of your mind, that you may prove what is that good and acceptable and perfect will of God."*

As we get deeper into this, it is important that we have an understanding of who we are in Christ. Before accepting Christ, we were slaves to sin; sin that was born out of our own fleshly desires. I want you to think about that for a minute. What does it mean to be a "slave to sin?" Exactly what is it that Jesus has set you free from? First, He delivered you from the penalty your sin deserved. Second, He desires to deliver you to abundant life that can only be found in Him. That does not mean a trouble free life but it does mean a life full of the abundance of God's grace and mercy. Jesus set you free from the law of sin and death. He broke the chains of bondage that held you captive to sin. You are no longer bound and defined by sin. You are no longer incapable of defeating sin in your life. You are no longer a slave, you are free; you are a new creature!

The Emancipation Proclamation, which legally freed the slaves in America, originated in 1863. However, it wasn't until

143

1955 that the freed slaves, as a whole, began to stand up and claim their freedom. It was a difficult struggle, but the freedoms, which they were fighting for, were finally obtained in 1964. If you do the math, from 1863 to 1955 is 92 years. So, why did it take 92 years for the freed slaves to stand up and claim what was rightfully theirs?

As people, we can do a lot to change the condition of another person's life. We can give food to the hungry; we can give shelter to the homeless and clothes to those who are without but the thing that is often the most difficult to change is a person's mindset. It is this mindset, this identity, which often keeps us trapped in bondage. The freed slaves had been in bondage for hundreds of years. They had been trained and taught to be slaves. Many had even been beaten into submission. Legal freedom may have changed their conditions but it did not change their mindset. My personal belief is that the 92 years between *The Emancipation Proclamation* and the Civil Rights Movement was a period of renewal, a renewing of the mind. It was not until the freed slaves began to see themselves as Americans and people with rights that they were able to claim what was rightfully theirs. By no means am I claiming to understand the hardships they faced. I have had the privilege of growing up during a time of relative peace and equality. What I am doing, however, is drawing your attention to the importance of the mindset of an individual that has been trapped in some sort of bondage. A similar conclusion could by drawn by observing the mindset of the children of Israel once they left the land of Egypt after

144

hundreds of years of slavery.

I believe that Christians go through the same process. Upon accepting Jesus as our Lord and Savior we *are* legally freed from the bondage of sin, no longer slaves. 2 Corinthians 5:17 tells us, *"Therefore if any man be in Christ, he is a new creature: old things are passed away; behold, all things are become new."* We are new creatures, no longer slaves to sin, but we also need to go through a renewal process. We need to renew our minds in Christ. We need to begin to see ourselves the way He see us. We need to stop living as though we are still slaves to sin and live as though we are free in Christ. Romans 8:1 says; *"There is therefore now no condemnation to them which are in Christ Jesus, who walk not after the flesh, but after the Spirit."* And therein lays the key. The key is to walk not after the flesh but after the Spirit. The flesh is what had us in bondage to sin but walking after the Spirit is the path to living free.

How do we walk after the Spirit? We pray and meditate on the Word of God. We obey His commandments and keep our eyes focused on Jesus, the author and finisher of our faith. We seek the Kingdom of God, which is righteousness, peace, and joy in the Holy Spirit, and allow God to handle the things that come into our lives to get us off track. We allow Jesus to renew our minds and we allow the Holy Spirit to cleanse us of all unrighteousness. This process is called sanctification. It is this process that brings us ever closer to our heavenly Father. This can only be done through a personal, intimate relationship with Him.

Consensual Christianity

I have had many people ask me why so many Christians seem to be just as caught up in sin as non-Christians. In each case I have seen, including my own, the root is always the lack of a personal relationship with God. It is for that very reason that I wrote this book, with the hope that it will help you see the importance of something that many believers take for granted. We have an open invitation into the presence of Almighty God, our heavenly Father, our Lord and Savior. We have one on one access to the Creator of heaven and earth. We are foolish to not take full advantage of this opportunity. Living free comes from living a life rooted and grounded in a relationship with God. God is not interested in religion or works; He is interested in a relationship. This is best illustrated for us is in Matthew 7:21-23:

"Not everyone that said to me, Lord, Lord, shall enter into the kingdom of heaven; but he that does the will of my Father which is in heaven. Many will say to me in that day, Lord, Lord, have we not prophesied in your name and in your name have cast out devils and in your name done many wonderful works? And then will I profess to them, I never knew you: depart from me, you that work iniquity."

Notice that Jesus did not deny the works they claimed to do. He denied knowing them. He said, "I never knew you. Sure, you took the time to do these works. You prophesied and you cast out demons; you did many wonderful works in my name, but you never took the time to get to know Me." God desires a personal relationship with you. Everything you do should be birthed out of this relationship and a desire to please your heavenly Father. We are no longer slaves to sin but servants of Christ. We are His disciples, called according to His will and committed to fulfilling His purpose. Live the life of freedom that God has called you to, the abundant life that Jesus came to give you. Jesus suffered and died for your freedom. Claiming what is rightfully yours starts with your relationship with Him.

Wrapping It Up...

Throughout this book we have discussed things like faith and trust; we have talked about the nature of God and His expectations of us. We have discussed stewardship, forgiveness, love, obedience and sin. We have covered a myriad of topics, so now it is time to take all that we've learned and apply it to our lives. It all starts where every good relationship starts; time and commitment. You have to spend time with God to get to know Him. Spending daily time in His word and prayer are essential to the life of every believer. The Bible is the single greatest resource you will ever have in life. Through it we learn about our God, His nature, His wants, His desires, His commandments, His passions and His virtues. As we read its pages we see His promises to us, His great power, His loving kindness, and His tender mercy. We serve a great God who has given us the perfect manual for a lifelong relationship with Him. It is imperative to our spiritual growth that we stay committed to spending time with our heavenly Father. Take the time to get to know your Lord and Savior but also take some time to get to know who you are in Him.

One of the single greatest mistakes people make, when it comes to their walk with God, is not having an understanding of who they are individually and who they are in Him. Learn your strengths and weakness so the Holy Spirit can guide you in applying His Word to your life. Knowing your strengths and weaknesses will also show you where you are most vulnerable to an attack from the enemy. Trust me, God will reveal to you who you truly are but it is up to you to take full advantage of His revelation. As God reveals Himself to you and He reveals you to yourself, take note of what He speaks to you. Take note of the things He impresses on your heart. If these things are important to God they should be important to you. I want to encourage you to keep a journal about the things you learn. Journaling is a great way to keep track of the places you've been in life, the lessons learned, and the things God has taught you.

God has a plan and a purpose for you. Part of that plan is relating to Him through prayer, praise and worship. Another part of that plan is sharing the good news of the Gospel of Jesus Christ with others as we are commanded to in the Great Commission. The third part of that plan, your specific instructions for life, will only come to you through spending time with the Father. There are things that God has commanded each of us to do individually and corporately but there are also some very special assignments that He has just for you. He will share those things with you when the time is right and your heart is ready. They could be as great as leading crusades that reach millions or as small as helping a single individual in need. Regardless of the magnitude in our eyes, they are equally important to God and to the lives of those you touch.

Also, be sensitive to the Holy Spirit. The Holy Spirit is our guide, our comforter, and our teacher. Look at everything in life as a teaching opportunity. As you spend more and more time in fellowship with the Father, you will become more in tune with the Holy Spirit who dwells on the inside of you. The Holy Spirit is your power for living. It is the Holy Spirit that enables you to stand against the attacks of the enemy and live a godly life in the midst of an ungodly world. Even Jesus required the power of the Holy Spirit to fulfill His task on earth. We see this in Luke 4:18-19 as Jesus reads from Isaiah 61, a prophecy about Himself, *"The Spirit of the Lord is upon me, because he hath anointed me to preach the gospel to the poor; he hath sent me to heal the brokenhearted, to preach deliverance to the captives, and recovering of sight to the blind, to set at liberty them that are bruised, to preach the acceptable year of the Lord."* The anointing is the Holy Spirit working through us. You and I are anointed to complete the tasks that God has predestined for us. In order for us to walk in that anointing, we must be led by the Spirit.

Trust God in all that you do. Know that God has a plan and a purpose for your life (Ephesians 2:10). Know that God is still Jehovah-Jireh, the Lord our provider. If His word says He will do it, He will do it; His word will never return void in your life. Know that you have been set free from the bondage that you were in. Sin is like a prison holding people captive but salvation is the key. Your freedom has been bought with a price, the Blood of Jesus. You are free from the chains of sin but you must choose to live a life of freedom in Christ instead of a life of slavery to sin. Remember to give thanks in all ways and for all things for you serve a God who cares for you and will never leave you or forsake you. He loves you, not because you have earned it but because of who He is. That means you can never lose His love. You can choose to refuse His love but you can never lose His love. So invest in yourself by spending time with God. He longs to spend time with you, He longs to share His plan with you, and He longs to share His love with you. We are not children without a Father; we are children of almighty God. Let's live the life of victory that truly reflects who our Father is.

My Prayer

Dear Heavenly Father, I pray that you bless your people. I pray that, regardless of where they are in their journey with You, whether they are newly born again or have been Christians for many years, I pray that you reward their diligence. I pray that you meet them where they are and shower them with Your' love. I pray that, as they seek You, they will find You; as they ask of You, You will freely give them what they ask according to Your will, Your plan, and Your purpose. I pray that, as they take time to develop a meaningful and lasting relationship with You, that You will reveal to them what You have revealed to me which is that there is love, hope, peace, joy, strength and comfort in You. Let them know that with You nothing is impossible but You are the God of all. Jesus, I thank you for your great sacrifice, for testifying to the truth, and for redeeming us and restoring the means of relationship between us and the Father, Your Father. Holy Spirit I thank you for teaching us, guiding us, protecting us, and directing us. Thank you for sealing us for the day of salvation. Thank you for giving us power for living. Help us to live lives that are totally devoted and pleasing to you. Jesus, it is in your holy and matchless name I pray. AMEN!

Final Thoughts…

If my life's journey has taught me one thing it is that there are no textbook, cookie cutter answers to most of life's problems and questions. God has designed us as unique individuals; we are all one of a kind. As such, our approach to things in life will vary, including our approach to a relationship with God. As my final challenge to you, I want to ask you to pursue God with reckless abandon. Seek Him with all of your heart and in your own way. Don't judge your relationship with Him based on someone else's standard but let His word be your litmus test. You are unique, love Him and know Him in your own unique way. There are some guidelines the Bible gives us to help govern our relationship with Him. We must remember that God is holy; He should be feared and respected. We must also remember that sin hinders our relationship with Him. Know that God desires a personal, intimate relationship with you. Not something that is spooky and mystical, but something that is authentic. Jesus said that God seeks true worshippers, those who will worship Him in spirit and in truth (John 4:24). That means He wants worshippers who don't hold back, but who truly present themselves as living sacrifices. Those who remember what God spoke through the Apostle Peter, "Be ye holy for I am holy" (I Peter 1:16). God knows that you and I are not perfect; He doesn't expect us to be. What He does expect, however, is for us to be willing and obedient; willing to submit to His will, willing to obey His word, and willing to allow Him to be our Shepherd. Enjoy your relationship with God. He enjoys being in relationship with you!

Thou art worthy, O Lord, to receive glory and honor and power: for thou hast created all things, and for thy pleasure they are and were created.

Revelation 4:11

J. Nathaniel Blizzard is available for book signings and speaking engagements. For more information, please contact Intrepid Ministries at (855)-775-2955